Ewha Old and New :
110 Years of History (1886-1996)

Ewha Old and New :
110 Years of History (1886-1996)

Edited by
Ewha Womans University Archives

Ewha Womans University Press

Ewha Old and New :
110 Years of History (1886-1996)

Edited by Ewha Womans University Archives

Copyright © 2005 by Ewha Womans University Press

All rights reserved. No reproduction, copy or transmission of this publication may be made without written permission.

First published 10 October, 2005
Published by Ewha Womans University Press
11-1 Daehyun-dong, Seodaemun-gu, Seoul, Korea 120-750
Tel. (82-2)3277-3164, 362-6076
Fax. (82-2)312-4312
E-mail : press@ewha.ac.kr
Online Bookstore : http://www.ewhapress.com

Price : 14,000won

ISBN 89-7300-655-X 03900

Ewha Old and New : 110 Years of History (1886-1996)

CONTENTS

President's Foreword ⋯⋯⋯⋯ 6
Preface ⋯⋯⋯⋯ 9

1. Ewha Haktang (1886-1910) ⋯⋯⋯⋯ 13
   The Dawning of a New Day ⋯⋯⋯⋯ 21
   A New Horizon for Modern Education of Women ⋯⋯⋯⋯ 24

2. The College at Ewha Haktang (1910-1925) ⋯⋯⋯⋯ 31
   Japanese Oppression and Ewha's Challenge ⋯⋯⋯⋯ 38
   Disseminating the Gospel as the Leading Women's Institution ⋯⋯⋯⋯ 45

3. Ewha College (1925-1945) ⋯⋯⋯⋯ 49
   The Establishment of Ewha College and the Struggle for Autonomy ⋯⋯⋯⋯ 58
   The Establishment of Ewha Culture and Curriculum ⋯⋯⋯⋯ 60
   The Heart of College Life : Student Activities ⋯⋯⋯⋯ 65
   A New Era Unfolds on the Shinchon Campus ⋯⋯⋯⋯ 67
   The Culmination of Ewha's First Fifty years :
      the Establishment of the Board of Trustees of Ewha Haktang ⋯⋯⋯⋯ 74

4. Ewha Becomes a University (1945-1961) ⋯⋯⋯⋯ 77
   Ewha Withstands the Turmoil of War ⋯⋯⋯⋯ 86

5. The Period of Growth (1961-1979) ⋯⋯⋯⋯ 89
   Ewha Progresses Amid Yearnings for Democracy ⋯⋯⋯⋯ 95
   "The Experimental University" and the Move toward Internationalization ⋯⋯⋯⋯ 98

6. The Take-off Period (1979-1990) : Reaping the Fruits of 100 Years ⋯⋯⋯⋯ 103
   The Great Stride Forward ⋯⋯⋯⋯ 109
   Introducing Modern Management for a Research-focused University ⋯⋯⋯⋯ 112
   The Centennial : Dreams, Fulfillment and Joy ⋯⋯⋯⋯ 117
   The First 100 Years and Renewed Commitment for Growth ⋯⋯⋯⋯ 119

7. Ewha-On the Road to Becoming a World-Renowned
   University in the 21st Century (1990-1996) ⋯⋯⋯⋯ 121
   Ewha's Vision and 100 Challenges ⋯⋯⋯⋯ 127
   Ewha in its Second Century : On the Road to Globalization ⋯⋯⋯⋯ 131
   The Grand Vision of Ewhaians : Helping Women to Shape the Future ⋯⋯⋯⋯ 142

Index ⋯⋯⋯⋯ 145

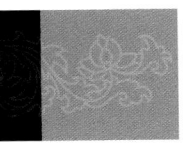

President's Foreword

The publication of *Ewha Old and New: 110 Years of History* is a joyous and meaningful event for Ewha as it looks forward to celebrating its 120th anniversary next year.

When we look back on Ewha's past history of 119 years, we are truly amazed at the great blessings of the Lord. 119 years ago, on a glorious day in the month of May, the Lord bestowed upon this nation a wonderful gift - Ewha. Throughout the following years, Ewha blossomed and grew into a great institution. But, more importantly, Ewha never failed to spiritually embody our nation's hopes and dreams for a better future.

While Ewha continued to grow during the past century, the world around us also progressed and changed. The velocity of progress and change accelerates with each passing day, and we are also being called to respond with equal speed. The forces of globalization that are transforming our world are compelling us to become "Ewha of the World," not just, "Ewha of Korea." Thus, the whole of Ewha is working hard to fulfill our mandate, and to establish and implement visions and strategies that proactively addresses the changing times.

In fact, it was back in the early '1990's that Ewha had the foresight to anticipate such changes and establish long-term development plans which

President's Foreword

have faithfully implemented. We became the first women's university to establish an engineering college and directly challenge the age-old gender-based division of role. We have also aggressively engaged in the research field of advanced sciences. As a result, numerous achievements were published and received world-wide recognition. Thus, Ewha has added a new face to its reputation : the leader in the field of science and engineering.

For several years in a row, we have been ranked among the highest in various domestic assessments and customer satisfaction surveys. Also Ewha ranked first in the Korean Council for University Education's Institutional Accreditation for the 1st term of 1995 and the 2nd term of 2004. Such high rankings are achieved consistently in individual discipline-level evaluations as well. All of this, I believe is the result of our hard work and dedication.

The newly published *Ewha Old and New: 110 Years of History*, is an English account of Ewha's history. It is the book that looks back on the achievements Ewha has made over the past century and how it has played a key role in the development of women's education in Korea by upholding the educational ideal of "realizing the human potential of women." The book also describes how Ewha has remained a firm pillar in Korea's rapidly developing and transforming society, how it has been at the forefront of innovation, and what initiatives are now being taken to realize its "21c vision" of "educating tomorrow's top women leaders of the world."

I am confident that *Ewha Old and New: 110 Years of History* will provide essential historical information and allow people from other countries to learn about the great strides that Ewha has made, of how it has now become the world's largest university, and of its vision of becoming one of the best private universities on the global scale.

Finally, I would like to express my sincere appreciation to the Director of the Ewha Womans University Archives, Dr. Bae-Yong Lee, for coordinating the project, Dr. Julie Choi, Professor Jean-young Lee and Professor Chang-hee Lee for translating the text into English, Dr. Young Choi, the Dean of the Graduate School of Translation and Interpretation, for the final proofreading, and all others as well as the many others who were involved in the process.

In-Ryung Shin
President of Ewha Womans University

Preface

In the year of 1886, the Year of *Byeong-sul* (丙戌) according to the Korean calendar, Ewha Haktang was founded as Korea's first all-women's educational institution. This marked the nascence of Ewha, and also of women's education in Korea as a whole. It was an important event in our modern history, well indicated by the event that followed the next year. In February of 1887, King Gojong bestowed the name "Ewha Haktang" (梨花學堂) upon the school through the Office for Extraordinary State Affairs (外衙門), and awarded a hanging board inscribed with the school's name. It was the first time for a modern private educational institution to receive its name from the royal court.

However, King Gojong's conferral of the school's name had a greater meaning than just that: it signified that Ewha was an officially recognized institution, comparable to the royal chartered private Confucian academies (*sa-ek-suwons*, 賜額書院) of the Joseon Dynasty. In short, despite being a private institution, Ewha gained the prestige corresponding to that of a national educational institution.

Another landmark event took place in 1946 which was again the Year of *Byeong-sul* 丙戌), as the full 60 year-cycle of the Korean calendar had passed since the founding of Ewha. This was the year that Ewha became the first university to be accredited by the Ministry of Education: a truly monumental event in the history of women's education in Korea. This event shows how the country recognized the educational achievements of Ewha and its role in the development of education in Korea.

As can be seen, the history of Ewha is not confined to Ewha alone, but is an integral part of the modern history of Korea, of Korean women, and of Korean education. And the newly published *Ewha Old and New: 110 Years of History* embodies the aspirations, dreams and vision of Korean women in the historical context of women's education in Korea.

Having already published *the 70 Years History of Ewha, the 80 Years History of Ewha* and *the 100 Years History of Ewha*, we are now publishing *the 110 years History of Ewha*. However, the advent of the global era necessitates communication on a global scale. That is why we are publishing Ewha's history in English for the first time. *Ewha Old and New: 110 Years of History*, the English version of Ewha's history will be instrumental in telling the Ewha story to the wider audience.

Another landmark event will take place in 2006, when the Year of *Byeong-sul* (丙戌) will come around marking the passing of two 60-year cycles. In commemoration of Ewha's 120th anniversary, the Ewha Haktang building will be restored to its original form with all the features of traditional Korean architecture. The restoration of the historic building will be a significant event for Ewha, not only by allowing us to take a retrospective view into the past, but also by letting others fully appreciate Ewha as a time-honored institution.

Preface

The publication of Ewha's 110-year history provided us with an invaluable opportunity to collect and compile the historical materials, and will serve as a starting point for future publications of Ewha's 120-year history, 130-year history and so on.

It is my sincere hope that *Ewha Old and New: 110 Years of History* will be a rich foundation for inspiring the continued progress of Ewha.

Finally, I'd like to thank the members of the Ewha 100-Year History Committee that provides with fundamental documents in this publication and the Ewha Womans University Archives for compiling materials for the original text, and also the faculty members who did the translation. I take this occasion to thank the staff of Ewha Womans University Press who has bent over backward to make this publication and especially thank to the director, Yong-Sook Kim.

Bae-Yong Lee
Director of Ewha Womans University Archives

Ewha Old and New : 110 Years of History (1886-1996)

I

Ewha Haktang
(1886-1910)

1. Ewha Haktang (1886-1910)

Mary F. Scranton, the First Principal (1886-1890) of Ewha Haktang

Ewha Haktang was established in 1886 by Mrs. Mary F. Scranton of the Women's Foreign Missionary Society of the Methodist Church in the United States. Under the motto of making Koreans better Koreans, she taught Korean students to take pride in things Korean rather than merely adapt to a foreign environment.

Ewha Old and New : 110 Years of History (1886-1996)

The First School Building of Ewha Haktang (1886)

1. Ewha Haktang (1886-1910)

Bogu Yeogwan (women only hospital)

A traditional Korean house on the premises of Ewha Haktang was remodeled into a hospital only for women in November 1888. Later, it was named Bogu Yeogwan (Building for Women's Protection and Relief) by King Gojong. At a time when nearly all doctors were men, the hospital's opening was like good news from the gospel to female patients because the strict social separation of men and women in Korean society meant that women could not generally receive needed medical treatment. Bogu Yeogwan began offering nursing education in 1903, laying the foundation for the establishment of the college of nursing and the medical college later. It was also a milestone in the modern history of Korean women in that it produced professional women.

Students during the Early Years of Ewha (ca. 1895)

Ewha began with young girls who had been neglected both at home and by society. The love of God shown through the founder, Mrs. Scranton, was the guiding salvation that awakened the consciousness of Korean women during what were hard times for women.

Ewha Old and New : 110 Years of History (1886-1996)

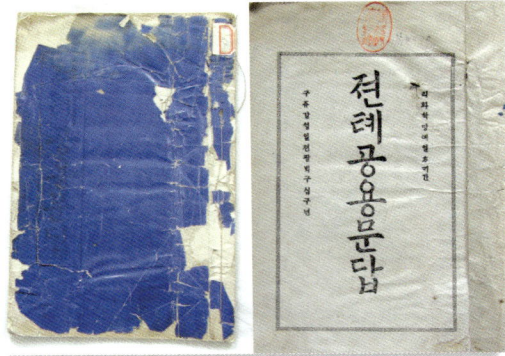

Lessons on the Human Body (1899)
This book, published by Ewha, was the first human physiology textbook in Korea.
(Soongsil University Korean Christian Museum)

Kimjang Vacation
(Holidays for Preparing Pickles for the Winter)
Nearly all Ewha students lived in the dormitory, and kimjang (preparing kimchi, or pickled vegetables, for the winter) was an important event for them since the school's founding. Every November, classes were suspended and the teachers and students participated in kimjang activities.

1. Ewha Haktang (1886-1910)

Wedding Day Was Graduating Day

When students reached certain age, teachers would find bridegrooms for them and marry them off. The teachers provided fully household goods to bride and bridegroom and also a bride's palanquin covered tiger skin up to drive out evil spirit. Students left Ewha upon marriage.

Meals in Ewha Haktang's Dormitory (ca.1907)

There were happy times for the students. All students lived in the dormitory.

19

Ewha Old and New : 110 Years of History (1886-1996)

Helen Choi, the 2nd May Queen (1909)
May queens at early Ewha were selected from among teachers, missionaries, and students of the graduating class on May Day, the founding day of Ewha. Helen Choi was the first student who was selected as a May queen.

A Visiting Day
Korean mothers wanted their daughters to seize a chance for making their lives better but they didn't.

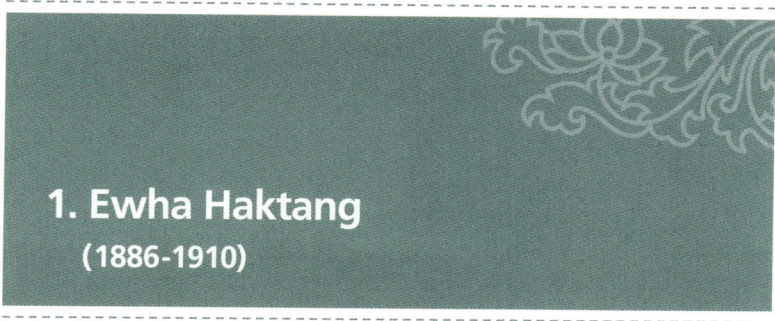

1. Ewha Haktang
(1886-1910)

The Dawning of a New Day

The Korean society of the 19th century was devastatingly patriarchal. Confined by their gender, Korean women dared not challenge the deeply rooted patriarchal authority and were inured to a life of endurance and suffering. They were denied the chance to study or to have any kind of social life. The most important thing in a woman's life was to get married, but marriage itself meant heartbreaking separation from parents and siblings, mistreatment by in-laws and oppressive household responsibilities. Under patriarchy, women existed simply as servants to men, and the value of their work was not recognized by society. Under such circumstances, women led extremely difficult and isolated lives, yet no one paid attention to the rights of women as human beings.

It was in the latter half of the 19th century that reformists began to take interest in the status and social education of women. Soo-jung Lee, an early Christian, sought to raise the status of women through Christianity. She sent a petition to an organization in the United States called the Women's Foreign Missionary Society (W.F.M.S.) in 1884, appealing for the dispatch of women missionaries to Korea. It was the prayer of a woman by the name of Mrs. L. B. Baldwin who drew the attention of W.F.M.S. to Korean women by making a prayer of offering for them at a local missionary service. It was her wish that Korean women achieve happiness through the words of God. Her prayers initiated the process that led to the education of women and introduction of medical services in Korea.

Foreigners's interest in Korea and the education of Korean women grew rapidly to match the fervor of Korean reformists, and missionary works were also stepped up. Books that provided an accurate and detailed account of life in Korea, such as Charles Dallet's *Introduction to the History of Korean Church* (published in 1874), *History of Chosun* (now spelled Joseon) (1880) by John Ross, and *Corea, the Hermit Nation* (1882) by William Elliot Griffith, shed light on the situation of Korean women and served as impetus for the education and missionary work for them.

Nineteenth century Joseon was plagued by political disorder, unending calamities and epidemic diseases. Farmers left their farmlands, and peasant uprisings occurred all over the country. Western powers continued to exert considerable pressure with the deployment of vessels and demands for commerce. But Joseon, under the rule of the Regent Heungseon (Daewongun), was obstinate in its adherence to the isolation policy and consequently failed to keep abreast with the changes occurring in the international society. Amid increasing external pressure and intensifying internal turmoil, popular demand grew strong for equality and freedom. Various schools of thoughts and social movements emerged during this period; most notable were *Donghak* (Eastern Learning), *Wijeong cheoksa* (movement to defend traditional values and reject foreign influences), and *Gaewha sasang* (Enlightenment thoughts). The proponents of *Gaewha sasang* were most eager to accept Christianity and called for the establishment of modern schools and education.

The founding of Ewha is closely associated with the introduction of the Protestant church into Korea. In 1832, Karl Gützlaff, a missionary from the

1. Ewha Haktang (1886-1910)

Netherlands, arrived in Korea and brought with him the Chinese language Bible. After the Korea-U.S. Treaty of Amity and Commerce was signed in March 1882, the American Protestant church became actively engaged in evangelical activities in Korea, and Horace N. Allen, an American pastor, arrived in September of 1884. The first official group of three Protestant missionaries arrived in Korea at Jemulpo (now Incheon) on April 5, 1885. The three American missionaries were the Methodist Henry Gerhard Appenzeller and his wife, and the Presbyterian Horace Grant Underwood. Meanwhile, the Women's Foreign Missionary Society (W.F.M.S.) of the Methodist Episcopal Church dispatched a woman by the name of Mary Fletcher Scranton to Korea.

Mary Scranton was born of Mary Benton on December 1, 1832, to the Rev. E. Benton, a Methodist pastor in Belchertown, Massachusetts, United States. The Bentons were the devout christian family that had produced three generations of pastors. She married William T. Scranton with whom she had a son, William B. Scranton. At the age of 40, she lost her husband and came to be ardently involved in missionary work as a staff member of the W.F.M.S. In October 1884, W.B. Scranton, volunteered and was appointed as a medical missionary, and his mother also became the Society's representative to Joseon. On February 1, 1885, Mary Scranton and her son's family departed for Korea. At the time, Joseon's socio-political situation was extremely unstable in the aftermaths of the *Gapsin Jeongbyeon*, a coup d'état staged by progressive forces in October 1884 to drive the Chinese presence out of the nation.

Scranton sojourned in Japan for some time before being reunited with her son's family at his home in Jeongdong in downtown Seoul on June 20, 1885. As she headed for Korean, Scranton firmly believed in the call and promise of God in her mission to Korea. Her mission was to establish an educational institution and to provide medical benefits for Korean girls who

23

had been fettered by convention. She ultimately wanted to guide Korean women to understand the love of God and to be reborn as new women.

A New Horizon for Modern Education of Women

General interest in women's education in Korea began to gain momentum around 1896 with the publication of the newspaper *Dongnip Shinmun(The Independent)*. Enlightened intellectuals stood up to work together and establish women's schools, and women began to take part in organized activities. Mary Scranton's contributions to women's education, however, preceded these efforts by a decade.

May 31, 1886, marks the founding of Ewha and the beginning of modern education for Korean women. It was a day when the door to education was officially opened to the Joseon women who were previously confined to a life of servitude and ignorance. It was the historical day that the women of Joseon found themselves standing at the threshold of a new era. Ewha Haktang and Mary Scranton played instrumental roles as pioneers of enlightenment and modern education for Korean women. Ewha Haktang opened a new horizon for the Korean women, giving them faith in their own abilities and independence. What made this possible was the Christian spirit of sacrifice and devotion, as well as the spirit of patriotism. The girls who entered Ewha Hakdang later grew up to become the leaders of the 20th century Korea.

The first student to walk through the doors of Ewha Haktang was a woman by the name of Kim, who was a concubine to a high-ranking government official. She wanted to learn English and work as an interpreter, but she left after three months. Then, at the end of June, a girl named Kkonnim entered the school and became the first permanent student. Her mother left her in the care of the school because she was too poor to support the girl. Kkon-nim was later joined by other girls, including Byeol-dan who had been abandoned by her parents, and Jeom-dong Kim who was to be later known as Dr. Esther Park, the first practitioner of Western medicine in Korea. She had came to join the school through her father who was working with Rev. Appenzeller.

In February 1887, King Gojong conferred the name "Ewha Haktang" to the school. There are many explanations given for the name Ewha, which means "pear blossom." The area surrounding Ewha Haktang was populated with numerous pear trees, and the hilly area where the school was situated used to be covered with beautiful pear blossoms in the spring. Thus, it was the natural surroundings of the school that gave it the name "Ewha."

Meanwhile, Mary Scranton was working hard trying to secure a site and construct a building to house Ewha Haktang. Finally, construction began in February 1886 and a building was constructed on a small area of 200 pyeong (600m^2) in Jeongdong, downtown Seoul. The traditional Korean-style house *hanok* building consisted of a few classrooms and a dormitory. At the time, the Jeongdong area was also home to the U.S. legation and missions of other countries that had been established after the signing of the 1882 Korea-U.S. Treaty of Amity and Commerce.

In the early days of Ewha Haktang, the rooms in the house served as classrooms during the day and as student dormitory rooms at night. At the time, all Ewha students were required to be resident students. So students would live in the dormitory for up to ten years and graduate upon marriage. For those early students, the school was like a home. At the edge of the tiled-roof house that served as the dormitory, was hung a small gong that was used to signal the beginning of the day. Breakfast was served at seven and classes were from eight in the morning to four in the afternoon. On weekends, the students attended services at Jeongdong Methodist Church.

Through communal life, students naturally acquired self-discipline and organizational abilities, and special fondness and friendship were shared between senior and junior students, which bonded them as members of the Ewha family. Despite many difficulties in the early days of Ewha Haktang, Scranton never gave up her belief in the all-girls' school.

She and the other missionaries were subjected to many hardships, but the greatest difficulty was the xenophobic attitude that Koreans held toward foreigners. At the time, the Joseon people regarded foreigners as objects of fear. People would run away when they saw foreigners on the streets and openly shunned them. There were no interpreters to make communication possible. Malicious rumors of foreigners made it difficult to recruit students, and the missionaries had to even sign memoranda to obtain the parents' consent in enrolling the students.

Amid such adverse conditions, however, Ewha continued to grow and prosper. On Oct. 31, 1887, Louisa Christina Rothweiler and Dr. Meta Howard came to Korea as a result of Scranton's earlier request for an educational missionary and female medical doctor. Louisa Rothweiler was an American of German descent, born in Detroit. She graduated from Wallace University and had abundant experience of working as a nursery and school teacher. She was appointed by the W.F.M.S. and taught Bible, elementary geography, and algebra at Ewha. In 1890, Meta Howard succeeded Mary Scranton and became the second principal of Ewha Haktang. Howard, a graduate of the medical college of Northwestern University, arrived in Korea in November 1888. Shortly after her arrival in Korea, she opened the "Bogu Yeogwan" at Ewha, a hospital exclusively for women, and established a training center for nurses.

One of the first students of Ewha Haktang was Esther Park. She was taught by Rosetta Sherwood and went on continuing her studies at the Baltimore Women's Medical College in New York. Upon her return to

Korea, she worked as a doctor at Bogu Yeogwan and offered medical services free, touring rural villages throughout the country. Coming from an ordinary background as a young girl originally named Jeom-dong Kim, she grew up to become Dr. Esther Park, the first Korean woman physician and a great philanthropist.

The training center for nurses and Bogu Yeogwan signified a significant period in the modern history of Korean women. Operating on the ideals of Christian love and care, the two institutions contributed greatly to the lives of Korean women. Bogu Yeogwan became the cornerstone that allowed Ewha to produce the first female doctor in the nation and to establish a medical college immediately after the nation's liberation from Japanese rule. Korean women at that time were inculcated with Confucian principles and refused to show their bodies to male physicians in any circumstances. As such, the opening of Bogu Yeogwan was a revolutionary event and a blessing for women in Korea.

In April of 1889, the first Korean woman was hired to teach at Ewha. She was Kyong-sook Lee, the daughter of a poor scholar in Hongseong, Chungcheong Province. She began working at the school after she has accepted the Christian faith through Scranton. Lee taught reading and writing in Korean. She was instrumental in publicizing Ewha to the general public and helped to dissipate the prejudices the public had against Ewha.

In 1892, Josephine O. Paine was appointed the third principal of Ewha Haktang. Born in Boston, Massachusetts, in 1869, Paine graduated from a teacher's training institute in New England and served as the principal of Ewha Haktang for 15 years. It was under her leadership that Ewha opened its middle school in 1904. She earned the affectionate nickname "father of the Haktang" for both her large frame and great generosity.

During the days of Ewha Haktang, the teachers were greatly assisted by other women missionaries or wives of missionaries in Korea. There was no fixed curriculum for the students in the early days, but by 1904, Ewha had reorganized the school and established a middle school with a complete and detailed four-year curriculum. This was the realization of a dream and the culmination of 18 years of hard work. The main subjects taught at the school included Korean language, mathematics, English, and Classical Chinese. From around 1900, the school began using textbooks that were written or translated by the teachers of the school. The first Korean physiology textbook titled *Lessons on the Human Body* was published, and textbooks such as *Political Geography* and *Natural Geography* were translated. Ewha was far ahead of the Korean government in compiling textbooks, and this fact shows that Ewha's education was substantial in content and also very progressive. These textbooks contained global perspectives, since they were either translations or revisions of American textbooks.

The educational ideal of Ewha was to free oppressed women through the Christian faith to allow them to lead fulfilling lives as human beings. The root of Ewha education was reviving the self-esteem and pride of Koreans. The Ewha founders wanted to help Koreans regain their dignity and to provide them with the right education. Ewhaians, armed with a new sense of identity, were able to realize their love for the nation and for their compatriots. The teachers at Ewha felt that there were no limits in the potential of Korean women. They taught the students with the aim of cultivating leaders of the future. It was such commitment and dedication that fueled Ewha's growth and made it into a university in such a short period of time.

From 1895, Ewha graduates began making inroads into all walks of the Korean society. The students of Ewha naturally inherited the lives of devotion and service from their missionary teachers, and the school did not neglect opening future opportunities for its graduates. The Protestant missions always incorporated educational and medical services directly into its evangelical work. This meant great opportunities were provided for Ewha graduates in many areas.

In 1896, the first tuition-paying student enrolled at Ewha. From this point on, students came to Ewha Haktang mainly to be educated, rather than to find refuge from their impoverished lives. At the time, a married woman visited Ewha, seeking admission. She was accepted in spite of school rules that banned the admission of married women. She had succeeded in persuading the educators by emphasizing that a mother had to be properly educated before she could carry out the education of her children. Her name was Ran-sa Hah, and she later became the first Korean woman to acquire a B. A. degree at Ohio Wesleyan University in the United States. After returning from her studies in America, she taught the younger generations at Ewha and became a famed leader both in the Christian community and in the society in general.

In 1897, new construction took place in order to accommodate the growing number of students. The Main Hall was completed in 1900, and the academic system was revised to become more structured. The Main Hall was a two-story Western-style red brick building with an auditorium and a dormitory. It provided appropriate space for cultural activities and functioned as a beautiful and safe sanctuary for learning.

In 1904, Ewha opened a four-year middle school under the government's authorization and drew up the first set of school regulations. The fact that Ewha opened the middle school before a elementary school clearly demonstrates, the fact that Ewha's primary goal was in higher education for women. In establishing the middle school, Ewha was also answering the pressing social need for teachers.

In 1908, Ewha also opened a primary school and a high school. Many graduates of Ewha returned and served as teachers, including graduates such as Grace Moon, Jessie Kim, Esther Choi, Helen Choi and many others.

Professors Me-re Hwang and Ran-sa Hah came to be recognized as leading educators of their time. Most graduates of Ewha middle school became teachers. The graduation of many middle school students precipitated the establishment of the college. Finally in 1910, a college was established at Ewha Haktang.

Ewha Old and New : 110 Years of History (1886-1996)

II

The College at Ewha Haktang
(1910-1925)

2. The College at Ewha Haktang (1910-1925)

Lulu E. Frey, the 4th Principal (1907-1921) of Ewha Haktang

She established the college at Ewha, the first of its kind in Korea. At a time when women married quite young, establishing a college to offer more educational opportunities to women was not an easy task. Producing female professionals, however, was the call of the time, and Ewha's establishment of the college in 1910 was the answer.

Ewha Old and New : 110 Years of History (1886-1996)

The 1st Graduation Ceremony of the College at Ewha Haktang

When Ewha established the women's college in 1910, the first such program in Korea, the public response was one of cynicism and skepticism. Society at large did not believe that women are really needed to go to college. The first students of the college at Ewha Haktang graduated in 1914, opening a new chapter in the history of Korean women. The three graduates (from left to right), Marcella Shin, Dorothy Lee, and Ae-shik Chung (a.k.a. Alice Kim), served as teachers at Ewha upon their graduation. Ae-shik Chung later studied Western music in the United States, the first Korean to do ever so, and became a prominent educator in Korea. She would go on to play a major role in establishing the Department of Music at Ewha.

Foundation of First Children's Education Program in Korea

Ewha Haktang established a kindergarten program in 1914 and opened Ewha Kindergarten Training School in the following year, pioneering preschool education in Korea.

2. The College at Ewha Haktang (1910-1925)

Twisting the Pole

It was one of the events held to celebrate the anniversary of the founding of Ewha. Students held the strings of five colors and moved in a circle to twist the strings around the pole. The team that made the most beautiful pole in the shortest time won the game.

Gymnastics with Professor Walter in the 1910s

As gymnastics was taken as a regular class, Miss Walter designed a gym skirt(*Jokki-hum*) for students which was much more conducive to athletics than the traditional female dress *Hanbok*, whose short jacket revealed the armpits when arms were raised and whose long skirt clamped the bust and draped over the feet. This was the first step toward redesigning the Hanbok, a bold innovation for that day, and the new Hanbok became common throughout the country over the years as more and more Ewha graduates went out into society.

Ewha Old and New : 110 Years of History (1886-1996)

Frey Hall, the Building Used Exclusively for 'the College at Ewha Haktang' (1923)

Ewha purchased the Sontag Hotel and used it as the college building until it was demolished. And then rebuilt it only for teaching lessons to college student in 1923. This new building was named Frey Hall, after the principal who opened the college.

2. The College at Ewha Haktang (1910-1925)

The Seven-member Evangelical Mission of Ewha

They took a leading role in enlightening the Korean people.

Ewha Chapel at Main Hall

As Ewha was founded on a Christian spirit, the chapel was an important part of school life.

2. The College at Ewha Haktang *
(1910-1925)

Japanese Oppression and Ewha's Challenge

Korea was invaded by imperialist Japan in 1910, and was subjected to thirty-five years of hardships and oppression under colonial rule. Japan seized Korea's sovereignty by mobilizing military power and forced Korea to sign the 1910 Treaty of Annexation. It then expropriated the land and property of the Korean people and attempted to control their everyday lives and thoughts. Most importantly, Japanese oppressed and controled educational institutions in order to annihilate the Korean national consciousness and force Koreans to submit to colonial rule. Higher education was discouraged by all means, and colleges were limited to providing a few vocational training courses. Moreover, in 1911, the "Rules on Private Schools" were introduced to control private education.

However, Ewha stood firmly on its Christian ideals and demonstrated a dauntless spirit that enabled it to overcome the oppressive reality. This

---

* As the official name in English both the college at the Ewha Haktang (1910-1925) and Ewha College (1925-1945) were designated Ewha College at that time. It's in need of comparting two those different schools with the former and the latter to avoid being confused.

strong would stemmed from Ewha's sense of mission to realize the freedom and progress of women. Despite such educational oppression of colonial Japan, Ewha opened a new era in women's higher education in 1910 with the establishment of the college. It was Principal Frey who first conceived the idea of a college, with the belief that women could be educated to become competent workers and visionary leaders. She wanted to provide higher education based on Christian values.

In 1911, Ewha Haktang had as much as 185 students enrolled in six programs. In 1912, "The Regulations of Ewha Haktang as a Private School" were introduced and two years later, on April 1, 1914, the first commencement of a women's college was held in Korea. It was a historical day not only for Ewha, but for all Korean women. The students who graduated on that day were Ae-shik Chung (Alice Kim), Marcella Shin and Dorothy Lee.

In 1913, a Japanese teacher came to teach at Ewha when the Japanese language was instituted as a regular subject, and Korean male professors taught Classical Chinese. Meanwhile, Ewha opened a kindergarten in 1914, and was also able to establish a Kindergarten Training School in 1915. This was the beginning of professional education for teachers. With the development of such academic courses, the number of students increased rapidly, and the Ewha Haktang college students suffered from a lack of space. In 1917, Ewha purchased the old Sontag Hotel and renovated it for students in the college and preparatory college course. Before the college began to produce a significant body of graduates, teachers who were former students of Ewha Haktang played an important role.

Graduates of the Ewha Haktang college included Ran-sa Hah, Eun-ra Lee, Helen Choi and Ae-shik Chung all returned to Ewha as teachers. Hah was the first to receive a bachelor's degree at Ohio Wesleyan University in the United States. She served as the head teacher and supervisor of the dormitory upon her return to Korea. Eun-ra Lee graduated from Japan's

Gatsui Women's School and taught music at Ewha. She continued her studies, receiving her M.A. degree from Boston University, and later served as a professor of music at Ewha. Helen Choi also graduated from the Gatsui Women's School and taught at Ewha. Ae-sik Chung, a member of the first group of Ewha College graduates and the first to receive formal music education in the United States, also returned to Ewha to teach.

The Western teachers who taught at Ewha included Principal Lulu E. Frey, Hulda A. Haenig, Grace Harmon, Olive F. Pye, A. Jeannette Walter and Charlotte Georgia Brown Lee. Grace Harmon had studied Bible and social work at the University of Chicago. She taught music at Ewha, providing systemized vocal lessons to students. Olive Pye, born in New York on November 28, 1888, had graduated from Smith College and volunteered as a missionary in 1911 after being inspired by a missionary's speech. She was the youngest of the missionaries, but she was extremely talented. At Ewha Haktang college, she taught science and art. A. Jeannette Walter, born in Latrobe, Pennsylvania, on February 3, 1885, was a graduate of Baker University, Northwestern University and Columbia Graduate School of Education. She taught mathematics in the college and was actively involved in school management.

After 10 years of numerous adjustments and improvements, the curriculum in 1920 covered nearly all of the major college subjects. The college curriculum consisted of Bible, English, mathematics, science, education, sewing, physical education, music, art, and Classical Chinese. Courses in geology, home management, infant care and cooking were subsequently added. The curriculum of 1920 shows that the preparatory college course placed great importance on liberal arts, science and mathematics, while the college program now provided more wide-ranging and in-depth education. Ewha's college program was aimed at opening wide the door to the world of knowledge for Korean women who had been restricted

2. The College at Ewha Haktang (1910-1925)

in educational opportunities. Ewha's English and music courses were particularly outstanding and deserved recognition.

Meanwhile, a significant amount of time was allocated to physical education for the balanced development of the students' bodies and minds. Women in traditional Korean society could never dream of stretching and exercising their bodies freely. For women to be truly free, they should have the control over their own body. But Korean women were constantly restricted in their movements by their long skirts and the tight skirt waists that wrapped around their breasts. Seeing this, professors Pye and Walter devised a gym skirt called *Jokki-hurri* to ease the discomfort of the students. The gym skirt (*Jokki-hurri*) brought about revolutionary changes in women's clothing, as it caught on even outside of Ewha and was popularized throughout the society.

In 1923, the construction of Frey Hall was completed. The college was the realization of Frey's dream, a dream that reflected her 27 years of dedication to the higher education of Korean women. Frey Hall was particularly meaningful, because it was the first building specifically built for the college. The building was completed and opened in September 1923, marking another important milestone in the history of women's education. As a modern building housing a dormitory for 150 students, classrooms and a library, Frey Hall was fully equipped with such facilities as running water and electric steam heating. The building was particularly significant in that Ewha teachers had done the architectural design.

Ewha trained students to become well-rounded individuals who could fulfill their respective roles in their society. Naturally, the students were encouraged to take part in voluntary extracurricular activities. Student organizations of the period pursued not only individual spiritual growth based on the Christian faith, but also strived to express God's love through action. This spread in the form of social volunteer work and joining the independence movement. As a consequence, many student associations were formed. The King's Daughters, organized in the fall of 1909, was a religious association that included every Ewha student as members.

The Missionary Society was a group organized in the 1910s and which still continues its activities today. It practices devotion to God through the love for other human beings. The Purity League, organized in the 1920s, sought a life of spiritual and moral purity in Jesus. The Devotion League was a devout religious club with a few dedicated members, including Professors Marie E. Church, In-duk Park, and Helen Kim.

The Seven-member Evangelical Mission of Ewha was founded on the commitment for spiritual growth and patriotic duty. The members (Aesiduk Hong, Hap-na Kim, Sung-duk Yoon, Pauline Kim, Ae-eun Kim, Shin-do Kim and Helen Kim) organized a nationwide tour to deliver God's words to Korean women who were suffering from ignorance and poverty.

Twenty-five years ago, Mary Scranton had begun such a tour to perform her evangelical duty. Now the young women of Ewha who had been her students were setting out to pursue the spiritual deliverance of the nation and its survival through faith. At times, they were persecuted by the Japanese police for their activities. They were nonetheless able to have five hundred people around the country who embrace Christianity. And because the students were able to witness the nation's sufferings first-hand, they returned to the school armed with a profound sense of historical obligation. Their activities thus set a path for other students to follow in the 1920s. Students at Ewha had always been eager to do volunteer work either on an individual basis or on a small-scale, but their activities became much more organized after the mission's tour. They launched Summer Bible Schools through which they could concentrate their efforts on enlightening rural farmers and delivering the words of God. Armed with the pioneer spirit and the willingness to love and serve, Ewhaians never failed to share the sufferings of the nation.

The *Imunhoe* that is Literary Society, was established with the aim of promoting students' intellectual and social capacities. The club held weekly meetings where the members discussed specific topics - mostly current issues or political events. Around the time of the Independence Movement of March 1, 1919, key leaders of the Literary Society formed a secret organization that acted as the central force in the students' movement against Japanese rule. Through such organizations, students were able to cultivate and demonstrate their individual abilities and talents, and develop their potentials as leaders. As the need for an autonomous coalition of student bodies grew, the Ewha Y.W.C.A. was launched as the official body that represented students' organizations. The Ewha Y.W.C.A. grew stronger, incorporating students' groups and their respective characteristics and activities.

The Ewha Haktang college which produced its first graduating class in 1914, had produced 29 graduates by 1925. The college graduates usually went into two different courses afterwards. Some students continued studying and acquired degrees to form the first generation of Korean women professionals. They returned to Ewha as members of the faculty. The second group of graduates took up leading roles in women's activities related to the Independence Movement.

The 1st graduating class, Ae-shik Chung, Marcella Shin and Dorothy Lee, worked as teachers and dedicated themselves to the Independence Movement. The 2nd graduating class, including Helen Choi and Me-re Kim, devoted themselves to women's organizations and missionary work. Helen Choi made significant contributions to the early activities of Ewha Alumnae Association. In-duk Park, a member of the 3rd graduating class, studied abroad and later established the In-duk College. Joon-ryeo Shin, a member of the 4th graduating class, committed her life to evangelical work after receiving her M.A. degree from abroad.

Helen Kim was a member of the 5th graduating class. She transferred from Young Hwa Primary School in Incheon to finish middle school, high school and college at Ewha. Throughout her student days at Ewha, she demonstrated exceptional academic ability. Kim received her M. A. degree in philosophy from Boston University in June 1925 and returned to Ewha as the Dean of the college. In 1931, upon the encouragement of Appenzeller, Helen Kim went to the U.S. and received her Ph.D. in philosophy from Columbia University. She was the first Korean woman to receive a doctorate. The theme of her thesis was *Rural Education for the Regeneration of Korea*. Kim was appointed the president of Ewha College in 1939, and she was appointed the president of Ewha Womans University in 1945 and served until 1961. She also served as Chairperson of Ewha Haktang Board of Trustees until 1970. During this time, she guided Ewha's growth into a world-class women's university. Kim manifested great talent in all areas encompassing women's education, politics, diplomacy and the Christian church, proving herself to be a new model of womanhood that led the times.

As members of the 6th graduating class, Bessie Lim, Bae-young Kim, Bok-soon Hah served as teachers. Esther Hwang, member of the 10th graduating class, organized the *Songjuk* (Pine-Bamboo) League and greatly contributed to the education of rural communities and the feminist movement. Salom Lee (Chung-song Ahn) played a key role in Korea's overseas Independence Movement, and Keum-bong Choi (Me-jee Choi) played a leading role in the organization of the Korean Patriotic Women's Society. Won-ju Kim who later became the Buddhist nun Ilyeop became a renowned figure as a woman writer in the history of modern Korean literature.

The Ewha Kindergarten Training School** had produced 98 graduates by 1927, when it was changed to Ewha Kindergarten Training School. These graduates went to all parts of the country to run church-affiliated kindergartens, laying the foundation for today's early childhood education. Among the graduates were Suh-rin Han, Bok-hee Kim, Han-na Yang, Sung-sil Kwak, Emma Kim and On-soon Hwang, Emma Kim taught the true essence of early childhood education through Ewha and established the model framework for teacher training. She was a pioneering leader in the fields of education, women's studies and Christianity.

Ewha's graduates worked hard to pave the way for women in Korea. As we look back on their lives, we can reaffirm the selfless pioneering spirit that Ewha instilled in them. These alumnae realized early on that women were also born as individuals deserving self-esteem and self-dignity, and presented themselves as examples for others to follow. They were pathfinders who made their way through untread roads. They responded to the nation's call for true leaders and shared the misfortunes of the hungry and the unlearned. They dedicated their lives to the cause of others, and the footsteps they leave behind are marked with pain and glory. It is through such brave young women that the spirit of Ewha could permeate every corner of Korea.

Disseminating the Gospel as the Leading Women's Institution

On March 18, 1921, Lulu E. Frey passed away. Ever since she arrived at Ewha in 1893 at the age of 25, Frey lived a life solely dedicated to Koreans.

** Officially named in English Ewha Kindergarten Training School has been reorganized of the educational system in three times. The first Ewha Kindergarten Training School (1-year curriculum) was the beginning of College of Education established in 1915 and the second Ewha Kindergarten Training School (2-year curriculum) was reshuffled in 1928. The last Ewha Kindergarten Taining School was rearranged to 3-year curriculum in 1940.

Ewha owes much of its early development to her untiring devotion. She was the one who established the college at Ewha Haktang and made college education a reality for Korean women. She also introduced kindergarten education to Korea and enhanced the quality of education at Ewha by recruiting many qualified teachers from in and outside Korea.

The Reverend Morris acknowledged Frey's contribution to Ewha at the cornerstone ceremony for Frey Hall by saying as follows: "One must acknowledge that today's Ewha is Professor Frey's creation. During a tumultuous period in Ewha history, Professor Frey insisted that education was the best possible solution for Korean women; and her views have been implemented in charting the course of Ewha's future. She conceived the idea for the college, and today we are merely standing on what she has achieved." Lulu E. Frey is remembered as the person who indeed set a solid foundation for Ewha.

In 1922, Alice Appenzeller succeeded Frey as the principal of Ewha Haktang. She was the daughter of Reverend Henry G. Appenzeller the first Protestant missionary arrived in Korea. She was also the first foreigner to be born in Korea. Henry Appenzeller established the Jeongdong Methodist Church and the Baejae Boys' School, the first Western-style school for boys. His achievements were important contributions to modern education in Korea. He also played a crucial role in the translation of the Bible into Korean. Traveling to Mokpo on a boat to attend a conference on June 12, 1902, he lost his own life trying to save others who were in danger of drowning, ending his 17 years of devoted service to Koreans.

It was that very same spirit of devotion and sacrifice that characterized Alice Appenzeller's childhood. She was educated at Wellesley College in the United States. While she was working as a teacher, she was appointed as a missionary to Korea by W.F.M.S. in 1914. She taught history and English at Ewha, then returned to the United States and received her M.A. degree

2. The College at Ewha Haktang (1910-1925)

from Columbia University in 1922 and an honorary Ph.D. from Boston University in 1937.

The most urgent task awaiting Appenzeller upon her return to Korea was upgrading the college into a full-fledged university. Under Principal Appenzeller's leadership, Ewha reached a new turning point. Ewha had long wanted to build an independent university campus. Members of the Ewha community prayed five years for a site to build a university campus in the Shinchon area. Their fervent prayers were answered in 1923.

On November 1, Professors Helen Kim and A. Jeannette Walter attended the World Women's Foreign Missionary Society executive meeting in Des Moines, Iowa, and submitted a formal request on behalf of Ewha for financial assistance. Professor Kim's gift to the W.F.M.S. museum was the gong that had been used to wake the students in the dormitory of Ewha Haktang. The offering of this gift showed the earnestness of Ewha's long-held hopes of constructing a university.

On that day, a very important guest was visiting Ewha in Korea. It was Philip H. Gray, a woman who was travelling around the world with her family to visit her missionary son. She came to Ewha on the recommendation of a Canadian woman missionary by the name of Saxe. Gray toured the campus and expressed much interest in Frey Hall and the work of the college. The leaders at Ewha explained the school's future plans for building a Christian women's university and showed Gray around the Shinchon area, then covered with wild pine forests. The Gray family made the decision to donate twenty-five thousand dollars for the purchase of the land, stipulating that no building be named after the family. Immediately upon returning to the United States, Philip Gray sent thirty thousand dollars and continued to donate as new buildings were added.

This was at a time when the Korean society was in dire need for a women's university, and the level of the college taught at Ewha Haktang was high enough to be incorporated into a full-fledged university curriculum. Moreover, in 1910, the Federation of Missionary Organizations had agreed to establish three Christian universities in Korea. However, the Japanese colonial government did not grant permission, as their "Joseon Education Decree" forbade the establishment of any educational institutions higher than the level of vocational colleges. Thus the plans of W.F.M.S. for a Christian women's university were thwarted, and Ewha was instead accredited as a college by the Japanese government.

Ewha Old and New : 110 Years of History (1886-1996)

III

Ewha College
(1925-1945)

3. Ewha College (1925-1945)

Dr. Alice R. Appenzeller, the 6th President (1922-1939)

She expanded the college at Ewha Haktang into full college in 1925 and opened the Departments of Literature, Music, and Home Economics to provide specialized education for Korean women. As the necessity arose to build new buildings to meet the increasing demand for higher education, she planned to move the campus and soon secured 60 acres at the school's present location in Shinchon.

Ewha Old and New : 110 Years of History (1886-1996)

Ewha Emblem in 1930   Ewha Emblem from 1945 to present

Ewha Emblem consisted of the color white, signifying purity, and the color green, signifying growth and prosperity. The two circles in the emblem represent the continuous revelations of God, and the gate in the center represents the spirit of Ewha, which was to open the way for the advancement of women in the wider society. The taegeuk (tai-chi) in the upper part is a symbol of Eastern thinking and represents the basic principle of the universe.

3. Ewha College (1925-1945)

Chemical Class in Laboratory for Practical Training (ca. 1930 in Frey Hall)

The Ewha College students learned the natural science such as chemistry, physics, physiology, bacteriology and so on. The curriculum focused on both theory and practice of natural science to support major courses.

Ewha's Early Interest in Korean Classical Music

Korean classical music was a regular class at the Department of Music of the Ewha College, a reflection of Ewha's interest in things Korean as early as 1930.

Modified Ceremony under the Japanese Colonial Rule not May Queen but Posture Queen (1934)

The May Queen pageant was discontinued due to intervention by the Japanese colonial government, and the Posture Queen was instead selected at the fall athletic meet from 1933 to 1936. A student with an upright posture and a gracious and balanced walk was dubbed Posture Queen. She wore a sash across her body saying Posture Queen.

To Systemize Physical Education at Ewha

Miss Stover, who had majored in physical education at New York University, made a great effort to systemize physical education at Ewha. After her arrival at Ewha, she designed an athletic outfit consisting of a white blouse and black bloomers. In the winter, she also turned the tennis court behind Frey Hall on the Jeongdong campus into an ice-skating rink by pouring water over it and letting it freeze. It was open to the students free of charge. This picture was taken in February 1935 to commemorate the last winter of classes at the Jeongdong campus.

3. Ewha College (1925-1945)

The Move to Shinchon Campus

On March 9, 1935, Ewha College and the Ewha Kindergarten Training School left the old Jeongdong campus and moved into the new Shinchon campus in 1935. In the last chapel service before Ewha relocated to the Shinchon campus, President Appenzeller gave a memorable speech: "Our Ewha is the crystallization of numerous people's prayers and love. There is no one-person that built Ewha: Ewha was born from the love of many throughout the world." The amazing power of prayer and love had made this miracle happen.

A Panoramic View of the Shinchon Campus

As the necessity arising from new building for higher education, she planned to move the campus. And soon she purchased some 60 acres in Shinchon, the school's present location. On May 31, 1935, the long-dreamed of Shinchon campus was dedicated. Now ensconced in the rolling hills of the Shinchon campus, Ewha began to fly high into the wide world.

Ewha Old and New : 110 Years of History (1886-1996)

The Staff of the Ewha Y.W.C.A. in 1935

Ewha Young Women's Christian Association was launched in November 1922. Before reorganizing as a department under Student Body in 1945 when Korea set free from Japanese colonial rule, Y.W.C.A. has substituted for students' association.

Once There Was a Princess

Dramas at Ewha began in Ewha Haktang with a club called the Literary Society. It put dramas in Korean onstage. In 1930, after the Ewha College was established, the Department of Literature began to regularly put on dramas in English. These English-language plays became a part of the history and tradition of the Department of English Language and Literature of Ewha University. This photo shows a scene of Once There Was a Princess, played in 1935.

3. Ewha College (1925-1945)

Inauguration for President Helen Kim
succeeding President A. R. Appenzeller Dr. Alice R. Appenzeller made circumspect preparations for transferring the presidency to Dr. Helen Kim in strong belief : 'Ewha must be run by one of the Ewhaian brought up by Ewha and necessarily by hand of Korea'. She entrusted Dr. Helen Kim who returned from study in America with a school superintendent and a vice principal. Finally Dr. Helen Kim became the first Korean President of Ewha history in 1939.

The Statue of Mrs. Chu Tae-kyoung (1943)

Although Ewha had been managed by the Women's Foreign Missionary Society of the Methodist Church in the United States since its founding, there was an increasing necessity to establish a foundation by the Korean people. At this juncture, Mrs. Chu Tae-kyoung from Jinju, South Gyeongsang Province, donated her entire fortune of 25,000 dollars at the age of 70 to fund the establishment of the Board of Trustees of Ewha Haktang.

3. Ewha College
(1925-1945)

The Establishment of Ewha College and the Struggle for Autonomy

The college program at Ewha Haktang officially became Ewha College on April 23, 1925. It initially consisted of a Department of Literature consisting of a one-year preparatory college course and a four-year college program, and a Department of Music with a one-year preparatory college course and a three-year college program. Shifting away from the previous focus on general education, Ewha College offered highly specialized training in the fields of literature and music.

Graduates of the Department of Literature contributed to the development of Korean literature and became leaders in the church and in various other sectors of society. The majority of the alumnae continued their studies abroad and became professors at Ewha. The Department of Music provided Korea's first practical training in Western music and also contributed to the development of traditional Korean music. There were about 70 students in the first year.

From the early days of the Haktang, Ewha had been offering home economics subjects such as sewing, embroidery, Western-style dress-making and cooking. The popularity of these subjects led to the establishment of the

Department of Home Economics in February 1929, and 32 students enrolled in the first year. Many of the first group of 18 graduates in 1933 became teachers in private schools. There were some who devoted their lives to the Christian mission, while others married and did their part to help improve and modernize the traditional family life of Korea.

The Ewha Kindergarten Training School, which had played a central role in the training of kindergarten teachers in Korea, expanded and became the Ewha Kindergarten Training School. As an independent entity, the institution provided an important training ground for kindergarten teachers, and offered a professional curriculum corresponding to its upgraded status. The Ewha Kindergarten Training School was able to extend Ewha's educational goals and philosophy on a broader scale. The curriculum consisted of liberal arts courses and advanced courses, and was very progressive in nature with great emphasis placed on practical on-site training at the three affiliated kindergartens.

Each academic year was organized into trimesters. The graduation ceremony took place around March 20, followed immediately by the matriculation ceremony. Ewha was a school open to free competition, and provided a structured academic program and curricula which made it the best possible educational institution for those who had academic aspirations. The school was ready to accept all those who had the desire to learn. Yet the actual number of enrolled students never reached full capacity, due to the lack of understanding of what college education was. However, when reviewing applicants, numbers were disregarded and all applicants were subjected to a strict screening process and examinations to ensure a proper level of scholastic aptitude.

Ewha's accreditation as a college brought many changes in the school administration. The most notable change was the formation of an alliance among missionary societies. By the 1930s, Ewha College had grown too large in size to be solely supported by W.F.M.S. and therefore, three missionary societies decided to participate collectively in Ewha's management. The Mission Board of the South Methodist Episcopal Church, the Canadian Presbyterian Church and the Australian Presbyterian Church have jointly been making donations to Ewha.

In addition, the increasing number of tuition-based students resulted in increased burden-sharing by Koreans in meeting the overhead costs of the school. In 1925, 25% of the school's total budget came from students' tuition and the remaining 75% was subsidized by missionary donations. Given the fact that less than 1% of the school budget came from tuition in 1920, the growth over five years was truly exponential. Ewha was beginning to stand on its own, and this increasing self-reliance also reflected the strong will of Koreans to be responsible for the education of their own children.

The Establishment of Ewha Culture and Curriculum

After 40 years of hard work, Ewha proudly established itself as the leading institution for women's education. It was now time to reach out and communicate the spirit of Ewha. In 1928, the students' organization published the first issue of *Ewha*. A 180-page medium octavo in Korean, Ewha did not fall short of a full-scope literary journal. The launch of the English newspaper, the *Ewha Weekly News Sheet*, around the same time was another important achievement. Considering that most college newspapers came into print in the 1950s, Ewha's efforts were both pioneering and creative.

In the 1930s, Ewha adopted the school emblem, the school motto of "Truth, Goodness and Beauty," and the Ewha school song through which it expressed its unique culture. The motto "Truth, Goodness and Beauty" reflected the dream that Ewha had pursued since its very founding, and there-in lay the combined ideals of intellect, virtue, and sensitivity. This remains the underlying educational principle of Ewha even today. It affirms Ewha's uniqueness and pride, and at the same time the nation's traditions and spiritual strength.

The school pin bearing the emblem was made of pure silver and consisted of the color white, signifying purity, and the color green, signifying growth and prosperity. The two circles in the emblem represent the continuous revelations of God, and the gate in the center represents the spirit of Ewha, which was to open the way for the advancement of women in the wider society. The *taegeuk* (tai-chi) in the upper part is a symbol of Eastern thinking and represents the basic principle of the universe. It is symbol also found in the national flag of Korea.

The lyrics and the score of the Ewha school song also embodied Ewha's spirit and ideals, and it was sung with heart-felt emotions on important occasions and gatherings. The music, which was in four-four time and reminiscent of a triumphant marching song, was prohibited during the Japanese rule. The Ewha school song (lyrics by Chung In-bo, score by Ahn Gi-young and Mary Young) consists of three verses. The first verse is about the founding of Ewha, the second verse is about its history, and the third is about the divine spirit of Christianity as practiced in Ewha, an institution established by God.

The ultimate goal of Ewha College was to provide students with the foundation to lead their lives as well-accomplished and exemplary Christians. Ewha worked toward a progressive restructuring of the school system, and effected many changes in curricular content and school policy. The joint faculty meeting of the Ewha College and Ewha Kindergarten Training School, held on September 3, 1932, presented the directions toward which the school was moving in the 1930s. Firstly, there was more emphasis placed on pragmatic subjects that could provide solutions to the Korea's economic problems - such as science, medical studies and education. Secondly, an integration of Eastern and Western cultures was sought. Thirdly, the creative thinking was emphasized. And fourthly, the school aimed at harmonious development of students that included physical, moral and intellectual aspects of their character. In a word, Ewha's educational philosophy was oriented toward a practical, creative, harmonious and comprehensive development of individuals.

Ewha's educational philosophy was manifested through school policies and curricula. Ewha College encouraged balanced development between the three departments: literature, music and home economics. Each program was composed of the combination of general requirement courses, major-related core subjects, and liberal arts courses. The general requirement courses were ethics, Japanese, physical education, and religious studies. Liberal arts courses were offered allowing students to access subjects outside of their majors, which was an innovative approach at that time. Among the liberal arts courses, physical education was especially emphasized, reflecting the school's focus on the balanced development of body and mind. Professor Myrta Stover established a full-fledged program and designed a uniform made up of a white shirt and black bloomer shorts. In 1930, with the appointment of Professor Shin-shil Kim, the physical education courses at Ewha reached another turning point. She introduced a variety of sports including women's basketball, softball, badminton, recreational games, gymnastics and modern dance.

Ewha, meanwhile, had been crowning a "May Queen" on its Foundation Day since 1908. This festive celebration, however, was temporarily disrupted during the Japanese colonial rule. So instead, Ewha held autumnal sports competitions during which a "Posture Queen" was selected. All Ewha students were taught to have beautiful bearing and upright postures - an element that distinguished Ewha students from others at the time. Ewha valued the beauty of a healthy mind and body, which requires continuous effort, over physical appearance which is beyond one's personal control.

The educational goals of the Department of Literature were to contribute to the creation of a new culture in Korea and to open a new chapter in modern Korean literature. The core courses were English, Korean, and Korean literature. Basic English skills were taught in the college preparatory course, while English literature was taught in the college program. In the 1930s, English drama became part of the established curriculum, contributing greatly to improving the quality of Korean theatre. In December 1931, Ewha opened the English Practice House at Hongpadong where the seniors of the Department of Literature lived with the missionary teachers and learned English in their daily lives. Since only English was used in the House, students could learn about Western customs and practice real-life English conversation.

Meanwhile, enthusiasm for the Korean language and literature did not wane. Although the Japanese prohibited both the use and the teaching of Korean language, Ewha's fervor for the Korean language never weakened. The passion for Korean literature at Ewha promoted national awareness and helped the people discover their true identity.

By nature of the discipline, the Department of Literature offered a wide array of courses. Great scholars of the time were invited as lecturers, and Ewha's students were exposed to the wide world of academia. Professor Marion Conrow was with Ewha for more than 40 years and taught English and pedagogy. Professor Catherine Baker, a poet, taught English poetry, music history and vocal music at Ewha, while Professor Velma H. Maynor taught English drama. The professors in the Department of Literature, such as Hyun-bae Choi, Eun-sang Lee, Young-ro Pyun, Hee-seung Lee, Tae-joon Lee, In-bo Chung and Sung-hee Lee, were some of the most accomplished Korean poets, authors, and scholars of their time.

History was taught by Professor Jung-hwan Cho, Rak-su Sung, and Nak-joon Paik. Professor Edna M. Van Fleet taught literary history and art history. The interest in Korean art history encouraged insight into Korean culture and fostered pride even during the period of colonization. Philosophy was taught by Chi-jin Han and Jong-hong Park, who organized the Research Club for Philosophy to enhance students' scholarly activities. Professor Moneta J. Troxel, Reverend In-young Kim and Professor Helen Kim gave lectures in religious studies.

The curriculum of the Music Department focused on both theory and practice of individual skills. The instrumental music majors received additional tutoring for developing techniques while vocal majors received rigorous voice lessons. It noteworthy that Korean music was included in the curriculum. This is meaningful as it encouraged students to appreciate traditional music and contributed to its revival. The Music Department also focused on music education and the training of music teachers. Education in the Music Department followed the American-style of one-on-one tutoring, and aimed at realizing individual characteristics and talents. In the early 1930s, the faculty was composed chiefly of missionary teachers. Professors Mary Young, Josephine Demeron, Catherine Baker, Eun-ra Lee, Alice Kim, Kyung-ho Park and Gi-young Ahn, had all been educated in the U.S. The professors of the later period, Sun-yop Chae, Won-bok Kim, Sang-hee Lim, Jong-tae Lee, Hwa-young Chung, Jung-sik Gae, Hoon-mo Chung, Jae-kyoung Hwang, Mary Kim, Young-ii Kim studied in Japan, the U.S. and Germany. They came to Ewha with diverse academic trainings and backgrounds and were mostly Ewha alumnae.

The Department of Home Economics taught students the science of home management, and provided academic training necessary to modernize the home. Major subjects included food, shelter and clothing, as well as other subjects related to health and science, and emphasis was placed on home management. Faculty members in the early days included Professor Harriett P. Morris, who had first established the Department, and Professors Hap-na Kim and Shin-young Pang. In 1933, the first class of the Department of Home Economics graduated, and many went on to become teachers. Ii-soon Choi, a graduate of the first class, was the first person to obtain a Master's degree and to teach at Ewha.

The faculty of Ewha College consisted of professors, assistant professors, and lecturers. Professors and assistant professors attended monthly faculty meetings. The number of faculty, which was 23 in 1925 when Ewha was accredited as Ewha College, increased to 37 in 1930. Among the 37 professors, there were 14 Westerners, 2 Japanese and 21 Koreans, among whom 6 were Ewha graduates.

The Heart of College Life : Student Activities

The Ewha Young Women's Christian Association Ewha Y.W.C.A. became the official autonomous student organization, as it embraced all the different student groups at Ewha. It played a significant role in putting Ewha's educational ideals into action. Student activities were organized by the Ewha Y.W.C.A.'s divisions for religion, literature, sports, rural community, social life, music, finance and missionary work.

The religion division emphasized volunteer service, while the literature division emphasized intellectual growth and social leadership. The sports division encouraged the development of a healthy body and soul; the rural community division supported the movement to enlighten farmers; and the missionary division supported missionaries at home and abroad. The social life division was responsible for creating an atmosphere conducive to a well-rounded student life. The music division contributed significantly to enhancing the reputation of the music education and activities at Ewha. The concert tours in rural areas were Ewha's special pride. The activities of the Ewha Y.W.C.A. the living embodiment of Ewha's ideals, were suspended in 1941 by order of the Japanese.

Life in the dormitory occupied more than half of the students' time in at school. In 1923, the dormitory in Frey Hall was completed, and the college students had their own dormitory for the first time. The students of Ewha were reputed to be modest yet stylish young ladies, and the Ewha campus was filled with their youthful vigor and intellect. Dormitory life was, and still is, filled with memories and romance. The lunar New Year's Day and the beginning of semesters were celebrated with parties where the students shared different regional customs by bringing food from their hometowns. The dormitory stayed open even during vacations, so that students could stay and receive private lessons or work at part-time jobs.

In those days, students wrote profusely, as indicated by the popularity of the literary journal *Ewha* which published the work of many students who later became well-known writers. Even romance also took place in the form of writing at the time. It was an innocent time when many love letters from outside admirers would find their way into the dormitory, and the young women on campus cherished literary dreams and youthful romance.

However, such romance was overshadowed by harsh reality, as participation in the patriotic movement took over the center stage of campus activities. During the 35-year Japanese rule, Koreans never ceased to struggle for independence. The March 1st Movement of 1919, the nationwide students' protest of 1929, and the protest by schoolgirls in Seoul of 1930 were some of the most outstanding patriotic outbursts of the times. Ewha students played key roles in all of these movements and a number of students were jailed as a result.

3. Ewha College (1925-1945)

A New Era Unfolds on the Shinchon Campus

Ewha had long fought to secure a space to build a university, and to provide a solid foundation for higher education for the coming generations of women. After registering as Ewha College, Ewha began to plan the construction of the Shinchon campus about two miles away from the original campus, and conducted a fund-raising campaign with the help of Methodist churches. President Appenzeller took the fund-raising campaign to America. The W.F.M.S. pledged US$60,000, and Mr. and Mrs. Henry G. Pfeiffer made a donation for the construction of the Administration Building. The U.S. $1,250 donated by Korean expatriates in the U.S. greatly encouraged President Appenzeller. Professors Helen Kim and Edna M. Van Fleet spearheaded the fund-raising campaign and held special prayer meetings in Korea to raise funds. The total sum raised by New Year's Day of 1932 amounted to U.S. $120,000.

This initial amount was not enough to even build two buildings. However, thanks to favorable changes in the currency exchange rate, Ewha was able to build several buildings with this money. Such a project would indeed have been inconceivable without the substantial contributions of Mr. and Mrs. Henry G. Pfeiffer, Mrs. Philip Hayward Gray, the South Methodist Church, Mr. G. Emerson, alumnae, professors and friends from around the world. Henry Pfeiffer was a devout member of the Methodist church, and a self-made businessman who lived in New York. Though he himself led a simple life, he contributed generously to the causes of education, religion and social work in many countries around the world. His wife, Mrs. Pfeiffer also supported construction of new college buildings for female students in Korea. Although she had never set foot on Korean soil, through her deep religious faith, she generously presented Korea with a university building.

The construction of the new campus began in September 1932. The new buildings were constructed not only of stone but also of prayers, sacrifice, ideals, hopes, and above all, the Christian faith. The Ada Prayer Room, the Auditorium, the Pfeiffer Hall that housed a library, the Case Hall of Music (present day Graduate School Building), the Emerson Chapel, and the Thomas Gymnasium were all erected on the new campus.

In the last chapel service before Ewha relocated to the Shinchon campus, President Appenzeller gave a memorable speech : "Our Ewha is the crystallization of numerous people's prayers and love. There is no one-person that built Ewha: Ewha was born from the love of many throughout the world." The amazing power of prayer and love had made this miracle happen.

On March 9, 1935, Ewha College and the Ewha Kindergarten Training School left the old Jeongdong campus and moved into the new Shinchon campus. Frey Hall and the other buildings of the Jeongdong campus were thereafter used exclusively by Ewha High School. A graduation ceremony was held on March 29, followed by entrance examinations the next day, and Ewha's new era in Shinchon began with the newly admitted students.

In 1935, Ewha celebrated its 49th anniversary. On foundation day, May 31, dedication ceremonies were held for the newly constructed buildings, the Pfeiffer Hall, the Case Hall of Music, the Emerson Chapel, and the Thomas Gymnasium. It was a big day for Ewhaians, and a day of celebration for all Korean women and the nation. The Clara Hall, the Jinsunmi Hall, the Home Management House, and the English Practice House were completed in 1936, the year marking Ewha's 50th anniversary. Professor C. I. McLaren planted cherry trees and ginkgo trees along the road that led from Pfeiffer Hall to the dormitory. These trees still stand today and have grown into a beautifully wooded area.

The completion of the Shinchon campus bears greater significance than mere expansion of physical space. Even the oppression of the educational policy of Japanese colonial rule could not halt Ewha's remarkable progress towards its goal of becoming a university. Though Ewha was registered as a college and not a university, Ewha never gave up its dream of becoming a full-scale university that embodied progressivism and academism as universities in the West. After 50 years at the Jeongdong campus, Ewha moved to the Shinchon campus with renewed commitment and far-reaching goals. The granite buildings erected on 65,000 pyeong (195,000m^2) of land marked an important milestone in Ewha history. The school made achievements in several areas in this period: emendation of school regulations, establishment of a complete curriculum, vigorous scientific research activities led by the "Academic Research Institute for Ewha College and Ewha Kindergarten Training School," and a significantly increased student body.

The revised school regulations were approved in April 1936, and the "The Regulations of Ewha College" and "The Regulations of Ewha Kindergarten Training School" were adopted. These new regulations were more specific and detailed than the ones they replaced. At the same time, the school system was overhauled. These changes can be seen in the "Ewha College and Ewha Kindergarten Training School Catalogue," published in 1937.

In the 1930s, forced by the Japanese colonial government, courses with nationalistic contents were reduced in number, and the Korean language and Classical Chinese courses were changed from compulsory to elective courses. In the midst of such changes, Ewha did its very best to enhance its educational quality as a college by strengthening major subjects. Ewha introduced the system of research students and the system of transferred students. The system of research students provided educational opportunities for those who wished to continue their studies after graduation and was a precursor to the system of post-graduate studies that was introduced after Korea's liberation from Japan. The System of transferred students admitted students through the transfer-examination to Ewha College. The system of selective course registrant allowed students to selectively sign up for courses offered by different departments. This system reflected the liberal educational atmosphere that respected students' wishes and opened new opportunities for learning. Korean students living overseas especially benefited from this system.

To foster an academic atmosphere on campus, the Academic Research Institute for Ewha College and Ewha Kindergarten Training School was launched in 1936. The Academic Research Institute, created to promote academic research, held monthly seminars. Different divisions of the Institute were assigned to pedagogical research, academic research and publishing, and all researchers presented papers and published reports. The research activities of the professors encouraged students to engage in more active research in their respective areas of study. The Departments of Literature and Music held monthly seminars to heighten students' academic interests and creativity. The seminars of the Literature Department focused on general academic research in literary topics. Professors, students, and graduates together formed nine different divisions and conducted research in their areas of interest. Other research groups included the Philosophical Research Club and the Academic Research Institute for Law and Economics. Ewha promoted research activities of professors and students on the campus and hosted many academic events outside the school.

The Ewha Museum opened in 1935, the same time Ewha moved to the new campus. The establishment of the museum was a landmark event in the history of college museums in Korea. Valuable artifacts were collected through collaboration between professors and students, and the students could learn the importance of history and culture through their access to the museum's holdings. Along with the museum, a college library was opened in the main building with over 16,000 volumes which were accessible to the students on an open-shelf basis.

On May 31, 1936, Ewha celebrated its 50th anniversary. For 50 years, Ewha had been a beacon of light shining through the darkness for Korean women. A commemoration ceremony was held on May 28 with the attendance of 700 students of the Ewha College, Ewha Kindergarten, Ewha Kindergarten Training School and Ewha High School, and 1,500 visitors. There was a profound sense of jubilation in the air as the 700 students, neatly dressed in white traditional Korean costume and braided hair, marched into the hall. President Appenzeller opened the congratulatory remarks with the following statement:

"I can feel your friendship towards Ewha and your trust in its future. We now wish to proceed with even greater faith and devotion towards the new age ahead of us."

A great many people sent unstinting love and generous gifts to Ewha. Some helped with gifts of the heart, some with time and money, and others with prayers. Many guests made congratulatory remarks. Seventeen professors were commended for serving the school for 15 years or longer. Ewha presented special gifts of rice cakes to thank the guests, adding to the festive mood. At the chapel service for the 50th anniversary celebration, Rev. Appenzeller emphasized hope, faith, and prayer as the strengths that made Ewha possible. For those who loved Ewha, there was no distinction between the East and the West, or man and woman. After the dedication ceremony for the newly constructed buildings, a play about the history of Ewha, "The River" was put on stage. The play was about a tiny spring that grew into a stream, then a river, and finally into an ocean, and symbolized Ewha's history.

As part of the 50th anniversary celebration, the busts of Mary F.

Scranton, Lulu E. Frey, and Philip H. Gray were unveiled. Ewha's half-centennial was an especially meaningful event, whereby the school renewed its commitment to social causes and the establishment of more progressive and practical educational goals, as a genuinely Korean educational institution. Ewha set forth with more determination than ever before.

The students who were educated at Ewha College sincerely sought to fulfill their roles in society. There were many people who automatically associated Ewha with an unmarried life, but Ewha graduates after the 1930s usually pursued ways to balance domestic life and professional career. Although finding employment was extremely difficult, more and more Ewha graduates were engaging in professional careers. The graduates of the Literature Department found jobs mainly in such sectors as education, including teaching positions at their *alma mater*, literary publishing, the Y.W.C.A. the church, the women's movement and social work.

Among the graduates of the Literature Department, were many well-known writers, including Yun-suk Mo, Chun-myung Noh, Sook-hee Jeon, Il-soon Kim, Choong-ryang Jung, and Sung-hee Kang. They formed the core of the Ewha Alumnae Writers' Association which is still active today with one hundred members. Other Literature Department graduates such as Ei-kyung Shin, Mary Kim, Maria Park, Hyun-kyong Cho, Eun-hae Park, Sun-hwa Choi, Joon-tae Gae, Kap-soon Kim, Jung-ok Kim and Pong-soon Lee remained as professors at Ewha. They formed the foundation upon which Ewha was able to grow into a university after Korea's national liberation.

In the areas of women's movement and social work, notable figures include I-kwon Choi, Jin-hae Kim, Shin-duk Choi, So-ran Lee, In-shil Sohn and Jung-sook Lee. They worked to create a brighter society by redressing sexual discrimination, economic disparity and social injustice. These graduates were Ewha's pride, and they contributed greatly to the development of Korea into a modern society.

3. Ewha College (1925-1945)

The Music Department at Ewha College elevated the status of music from a subject once held in contempt by the Korean society to that of art which is loved and respected by the public. The Department produced many professional performers, including numerous pianists, Korea's first woman composer Soon-ae Kim, and vocalists Sun-yop Chae and Ja-kyoung Kim. Ja-kyoung Kim, who had performed at Carnegie Hall, founded Korea's first opera company which continues to be a figurehead of Korean opera today. And numerous graduates of Ewha became high school teachers and college professors.

The Department of Home Economics changed the role of the homemaker. Instead of being the traditionally dutiful and submissive housewife, the modern woman was being called to manage the home and be responsible for home economics by taking a scientific approach to childcare, food, clothing, housing, health and financial matters. Such an approach based on rationalism and efficiency revolutionized women's consciousness and gave them a broader outlook on society. The graduates of the Ewha Home Economics Department formed the mainstay of the discipline in Korea. Ii-Soon Choi returned from her studies abroad and established the Home Economics Department at Yonsei University. Tae-young Lee started out as a major in Home Economics, but studied law after developing an interest in law and economics in college, and later became the first woman lawyer in Korea.

Almost all of the graduates of Ewha Kindergarten Training School became kindergarten teachers. Kindergarten education was conceived on hopes for a brighter future for the nation, and Ewha graduates helped turn these hopes into reality.

Ewha's educational goal was to educate future leaders who could lead fulfilling lives and share with neighbors in the spirit of Christianity. The graduates of Ewha lived up to these goals both in the home and at the workplace. Owing to them, Ewha remained a source of hope in the dismal days of colonial rule. Also to be remembered were the countless Ewha graduates whose names were not recorded, but who silently and faithfully performed their duties wherever they were.

The Culmination of Ewha's First Fifty years: the Establishment of the Board of Trustees of Ewha Haktang

At that time, new adjustments were made in the school system. Ewha Kindergarten Traning School became a three-year program and a one-year program in Home Management was newly established. Due to Japanese intervention, the curriculum was changed to offer more courses in Japanese Studies, while courses in Korean language and Classical Chinese were completely eliminated.

The year 1938 marked a new chapter in the history of Ewha as an Ewha graduate took charge of the school administration for the first time in 53 years. Professor Helen Kim was inaugurated as President of Ewha College. Many Korean leaders had come to realize that they should not simply rely on foreigners to run the country's leading institution for women's education. In the spring of 1921, a Korean-American Cooperative Board of Trustees was formed at Ewha Haktang and Koreans were finally able to take part in the management of Ewha. The Missionary Society had always wanted to delegate the management to Koreans, and the transition accelerated in the 1930s.

Leaders from all walks of Korean society, including educational and religious sectors, came together and formed the Supporters' Association for Ewha College. In answer to the active participation and financial support of Korean leaders, the school changed its management policy from "Ewha

College of the Christian Missionary Association" to "Ewha College by the Korean People for the Korean Society." This was a major transition that provided a foundation for true independence.

However, Ewha did not stop there. It reaffirmed the commitment to grow into a university, and become a true institution of higher learning for Korean women. The inaugural meeting of the Supporters' Association for Ewha College was held at the auditorium of Ewha College in Jeongdong in February 1933. Twenty-five council members were elected. In an attempt to control the country's education, Japan exerted pressure and ordered that all contributions to private schools be stopped. But in 1943, Ewha successfully launched the Board of Trustees composed of 11 trustees and 2 auditors under the leadership of Dr. Helen Kim and an inaugural fund of U.S. $500,000.

The creation of the Board of Trustees of Ewha Haktang was nothing short of a miracle, considering that only 50 years ago the school was unable to even pay for its overhead costs. The Board could be launched because of the devoted efforts of Korean leaders who had shared the belief that education was the only way to salvage the nation. Two donors worth special mention were Tae-kyoung Chu, a widow who donated her whole life's savings of U.S. $25,000, and Chang-sik Sohn, a businessman living in China, who donated a sum of U.S. $125,000.

By 1936, Japan's colonial government was growing even more oppressive. The Japanese forced its State Shintoism on Koreans and persecuted Christian schools and the Korean church. Many Christian private schools were closed for refusing to worship the Shinto shrine. Ewha agreed to worship the Shinto shrine in order to protect the school, but many hardships ensued. As the conflict between the Christian church, missionaries, and the Japanese intensified, missionaries started to return to their home countries. This included people like Wood, Conrow, Morris, Hulbert, Young, Baker and Appenzeller who had all served as professors for many years at Ewha and regarded Ewha as their home. The hearts of Ewhaians were filled with sadness and remorse as they watched the missionaries and teachers leave. Their departure was a grave trial for Ewha, but the moment also marked the beginning of Ewha's self-reliance. Ewha had to learn to stand firmly on its own in times of great despair.

The Japanese oppression mounted, leading to the sudden order in 1944 to abolish all college programs. Ewha was forced to reduced its curriculum to a one-year program called Leadership Training for Young Women. Japan took even more oppressive measures and dispatched inspectors to the school, dismissed professors in large numbers and forced the school to change its name to "Gyeongseong Women's College."

But Ewha endured the situation undaunted. Ewha took over the management of Dongdaemoon Women's Hospital, which later served as the basis for the Department of Medicine at the school after Korea's liberation. Ewha remained true to its calling as the only educational institution of higher learning for Korean women. Ewha had the duty to proclaim the love and righteousness of Jesus especially because so many other educational institutions were being forced to close down. Ewha did not fail in this duty.

Ewha Old and New : 110 Years of History (1886-1996)

IV

Ewha Becomes a University
(1945-1961)

4. Ewha Becomes a University (1945-1961)

Dr. Helen Kim, the 7th President (1939-1961)

She became the first Korean female Ph.D. when she received a doctor of philosophy degree from Columbia University in 1931. She was the first graduate of Ewha and also the first Korean to become president of Ewha when she became the school's 7th president in 1939. She continued to serve as president after Ewha became a university in 1946.

Ewha Old and New : 110 Years of History (1886-1996)

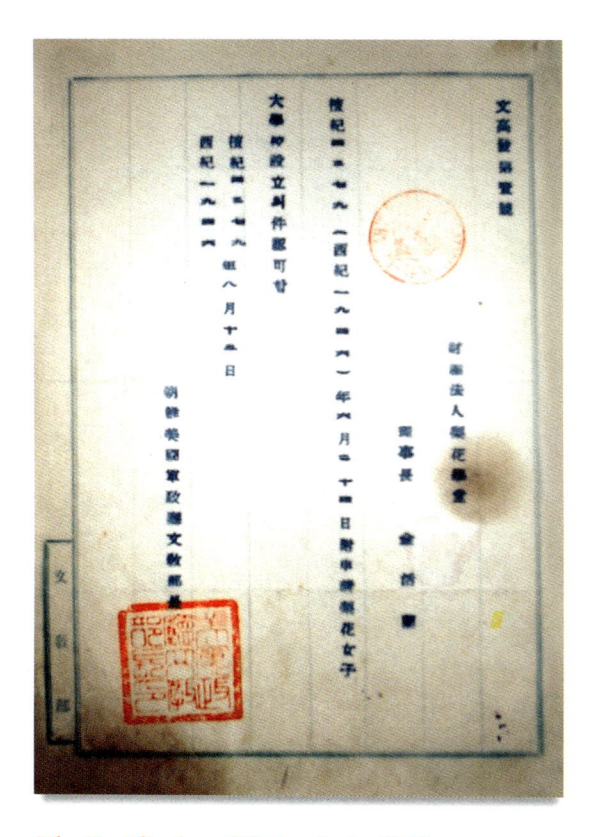

The Certification of University in 1946
University Certificate issued by the Ministry of Education (1946). The era of Ewha as a university began.

4. Ewha Becomes a University (1945-1961)

Busan Evacuee Campus

Even chaotic state caused by the Korean War, Ewha built a school building in Bumin-dong, Busan, where it evacuated and continued to uphold the ideals of scholarship, giving hope and courage to many people who were weary of life as evacuees.

Graduation at Evacuee Campus of Busan

Ewha advertised the opening of the Evacuee campus in Busan through daily newspapers and urged students to continue their studies, seeing some 100 students graduated in 1953.

81

Ewha Old and New : 110 Years of History (1886-1996)

The First Women's Graduate School and the First Female Masters in Korea

Ewha established Korea's first women's Graduate School in March 1950 to cultivate female leadership and creativity in academia. The photo shows the students of the 1st graduating class of the Graduate School in 1954. Ewha continued to offer instruction even during the Korean War, and it produced the first female masters in Korea right after the war.

4. Ewha Becomes a University (1945-1961)

Welch-Ryang Auditorium

In commemoration of the 70th anniversary of its foundation in 1956, Ewha dedicated 4,000-person capacity Welch-Ryang Auditorium.

4. Ewha Becomes a University
(1945-1961)

Korea was liberated on August 15, 1945, when Japan was defeated in World War II. But even before the euphoria of national liberation was over, the Korean peninsula was partitioned by the U.S. and Soviet Union at the 38th parallel and was placed under trusteeship. On September 8, 1945, the U.S. forces arrived in South Korea and governed the country by military rule. The U.S. Bureau of School Affairs was established and announced the resumption of education above the level of elementary and middle school. The most visible development after liberation was seen in the area of women's education. Amid rapidly growing demand for women's higher education, Ewha was able to resume growth and became a university.

Even under the worst of the Japanese oppression, Ewha's Korean President, Helen Kim and other professors such as Emma Kim, Young-Ii Kim, Okgill Kim, Jung-ae Lee, Joon-sup Kim, Jung-koo Lee, Kwan-yol Ryoo, Il-sun Yoon, In-sup Chung, and Hee-deuk Won had devoted themselves to the continued development of Ewha. Ewha submitted its petition to be promoted to the status of university and reorganized the school into specialized departments and college departments. Thanks to President Helen Kim's careful stewardship, the school did not experience any disruption at the time of liberation. The oppressive colonial situation had not barred Ewha from steadily preparing its future as a university.

4. Ewha Becomes a University (1945-1961)

On October 1, 1945, Ewha assumed its new name "Ewha Womans University," as it became the first university to be officially recognized by the Ministry of Education. This was a moment portending the bright future of Korean women. To be upgraded as a university, Ewha went through the process of new student admission, first entrance examinations, government accreditation, and the transfer of students from the old college to the new university. The new university structure heightened Ewha's prestige.

When the official license of full university was granted on August 15, 1946, Ewha had three separate colleges : Medicine, Art, and Academics. The College of Academics was composed of the Departments of Literature, Home Economics, Physical Education, Education, and Early Childhood Education. The College of Art had the Departments of Music and of Fine Arts, while the College of Medicine had two departments, Department of Medicine and Department of pharmacy. The educational objectives of those departments were to train students into women leaders of spirit and ability, who could contribute to the development of the nation and society based on Christian ideals.

Between 1945 and 1950, the foundation of the new university was laid. Because of the sudden increase in the number of students, Ewha had to concentrate its efforts on the creation of new facilities and expansion of space. Meanwhile, the missionary teachers who had been forced to leave the country during the final years of Japanese rule, returned to Ewha. There were also other important developments such as the revision of the curriculum, an increase in the number of professors, overseas research, expansion of the library collection, opening of the affiliated hospital, establishment of the Graduate School, launching of the Ewha University Press and revival of the *Ewha* journal.

On February 20, 1950, while leading chapel services, Appenzeller was hit by a stroke and passed away. Born and buried in Korea, the sixty-six years of her entire life was one of single-minded devotion to Korean women and

Ewha. She was an inspiration during her lifetime, and her love and passion for Ewha will always be cherished in the hearts of Ewhaians. The Science Hall, completed in 1955, was named "Appenzeller Hall" in her memory.

Ewha Withstands the Turmoil of War

At the crack of dawn on June 25, 1950, the communist army of North Korea invaded South Korea and triggered the Korean War. The war which lasted for three years and one month until an armistice was signed on July 27, 1953 was the most tragic national ordeal. Recognizing the urgency of the situation, Ewha closed the school on June 27, and sent all the boarding students home. Then the faculty and students followed the government and evacuated to Busan.

After the retreat of January 4, 1951, the armistice negotiation started to take place, during which the war front became entrenched. The Ministry of Education put forward a wartime policy establishing a union of colleges in anticipation of a protracted war. In January 1951, the newspapers advertised the call for the return of Ewha professors, and in February, Ewha partially joined the wartime union of colleges. In the end, Ewha decided to re-open the school, with the intention of taking responsibility of its own students. It was a daring thought since the war was raging on and financial resources were scarce.

In August 1951, Ewha opened its "Evacuee campus" by putting up tents as makeshift buildings on a leased site in Bumindong, Busan. The graduate school was refounded. The number of students who enrolled at the Evacuee campus reached 859. A dedication ceremony was held on December 8, 1951. Ewha's first academic journal *Educational Research* was inaugurated at the

4. Ewha Becomes a University (1945-1961)

Evacuee campus and on October 7, 1951, Ewha became the first private university to establish a College of Education in Korea. In April 1952, the College of Law was founded, and diverse cultural events such as drama performances and concerts were held to commemorate the event. Conditions were difficult, as classes were being held in makeshift buildings that were tented structures, but neither the pain of war nor the dire conditions could dampen the passion for learning. Life in general was hard due to the serious shortage in commodities, and Ewha students were no exception. "Friends of Ewha" a supporters' group in Kansas, the hometown of the women missionaries named H. P. Morris and A. Jeannette Walter, sent relief goods that helped many at Ewha.

When the Armistice was signed, Ewha began the process of reconstruction. Ewha's history and spirit had resolutely survived the havoc of war and returned to Seoul. On September 1, 1953, Ewha reopened the school. The biggest challenges at the time were repairing and restoring the buildings and facilities and reopening the courses. With the support of both Koreans and foreigners, reconstruction proceeded rapidly. In 1957, the Welch-Ryang Auditorium was built; in 1958, the Ewha Bridge, the athletics field, Billingsley Hall and the library (present day Helen Hall) were built; and in 1960, the Museum and the Korean-American Hall (Hakkwan) opened. The Ewha campus was rapidly expanding becoming a grand in scale.

The number of students increased every year and reached 6,527 in 1958, with 309 professors and 124 administration personnel. Professors were provided with offices and overseas training opportunities. The Committee for Faculty Promotion was established to support faculty research activities. Furthermore, the Department of General Education was created to strengthen liberal arts education. The Graduate School which had been forced to close down by the war only two weeks after its opening, had been reinstated at the Evacuee campus in Busan. The graduate program resumed in earnest after returning to Seoul. In 1954, the Graduate School produced its first five graduates.

In the latter half of 1950s, the Korean Cultural Research Institute was established as an independent research center to spearhead faculty research, particularly on the interpretation and preservation of Korea's unique culture and tradition. On February 12, 1954, the long-awaited university paper the *Edae Hakbo* (Weekly Ewha) was first published. Its purpose was to communicate school information, provide quality information, contribute to daily life of student and promote sound public opinion. The *Ewha Voice* (English-language university paper) was first issued on June 10, 1954.

On May 31, 1956, Ewha celebrated its 70th anniversary. Ewha had now grown into a university of about 4,800 students and 300 faculty members. For the celebration, the following events were planned: the Pageant of the May Queen, a large-scale Christian revival meeting, the commendation of faculty and staffs who had served for long periods at Ewha, the publication of a collection of essays commemorating the anniversary, compilation of Ewha's 70-year history, drama, opera performances and exhibitions. The construction of the Welch-Ryang Auditorium was also planned.

On May 31, 1956, President Helen Kim expressed her emotions and future hopes for Ewha by declaring, "Ewha's struggle is something more than a simple educational movement. It is a women's liberation movement. We shall not follow the flow of the times, the times shall follow us." Ewha's 70-year history was lauded even by those outside the university as having greatly contributed to the promotion of women's social status in Korea.

Ewha Old and New : 110 Years of History (1886-1996)

V

The Period of Growth
(1961-1979)

5. The Period of Growth (1961-1979)

Kim Okgill, the 8th President (1961-1979)

She expanded the enrollment of students from some 5,000 when she took office in 1961 to 8,000 and worked out ten-year development plan to address the damage from the war and reestablish school management.

Mass Game for Commemorating the 80th Anniversary of Ewha (1966)

5. The Period of Growth (1961-1979)

A Pioneer in the Women's Studies in Korea

Standing at the vanguard of women's higher education in Korea, Ewha has advanced without rest to help create an equal, gender discrimination-free society and promote the self-actualization of the women of the world. Opening Korea's first women's studies program in 1977, Ewha has spared no efforts to realize equal treatment of women in both theory and practice. Having written the history of Korean women with an awakened spirit, Ewha has fulfilled its role as the center of the feminist movement in Korea by presenting a forward-looking image of women.

The 1970s and 1980s Were Tainted by Various Conflicts in the Korean Society.

The academia was the center of the strongest resistance against authoritarianism and military dictatorship. Ewha was not an exception. Ewha never abandoned its Christian values, its idea of women's liberation and its dream to contribute to the nation. In this context, Ewha was even more active than other universities. The students' thirst for democracy and social justice were expressed through demonstrations, student debates, special lectures and drama performances.

5. The Period of Growth
(1961-1979)

Ewha Progresses Amid Yearnings for Democracy

Korea underwent immense political and social change in the 1960s. On April 19, 1960, the students of the nation rallied for democracy and protested against the deap-seated corruption of President Rhee Syng-man's government and the rigged presidential and vice-presidential elections. With the April Uprising, the Rhee Syng-man government collapsed and the demand for democracy grew stronger. The central figures of April 19 movement were college students and intellectuals, and universities were in the middle of the overriding demand for reforms.

However, with the military coup d'etat of May 16, 1961, universities had to face another wave of great change. After the coup, the new government implemented the University Restructuring Law. In accordance with the provisions of the new statute, certain university departments were closed and the overall number of university students was drastically decreased. Universities lost their rights to confer degrees on their graduates and, instead, the government conducted a nationwide test qualifying bachelor's degree holders. Furthermore, the government lowered the professors' retirement age to 60, and President Helen Kim had to step down from her presidency.

The inaugural ceremony of President Kim Okgill was held on September 30, 1961. The departing president Helen Kim said in her farewell address, "The best is yet to come, and for that, this is a beginning. I promise that even after I retire, I will continue to do my utmost to achieve our common goal." Her words, a pledge to unrelenting progress and a reaffirmation of continued devotion, touched the hearts of many Ewhaians.

In her inaugural speech, the new President Kim Okgill said: "The most significant feature of Ewha was the training of women leaders dedicated to Christian values." Under the new president, Ewha once again embarked upon the road to creating history. This was not a transition but a succession. Ewha's history, rooted in Christianity and the Korean national spirit, had always borne the responsibility of fostering women leaders in an endless strive for progress.

Helen Kim's presidency, from 1939 to 1961, were tumultuous years, but Ewha had managed to proceed along an astonishing track of progress. And the person who had led Ewha through the thorny path was no other than President Helen Kim. Her life is synonymous to Ewha history. She was someone that Ewha had produced and who in turn produced Ewha.

Ewha's eighth president, Kim Okgill, was a typical Ewhaian, someone who had grown up, studied, and developed her will and spirit at Ewha. Born on March 10, 1921, in Maengsan, South Pyongan province in what is now north Korea, she graduated from the Literature Department of Ewha College in 1943, studied Christianity at Wesleyan University and Educational Administration at the Graduate School of Temple University in the United States. Throughout the bleak years of Japanese rule, post-liberation confusion and the ruins of war, she studied, taught, and served at Ewha. Upon the foundation of the past, she was to provide fresh energy for Ewha's continued development.

By its 80th anniversary in 1966, Ewha had matured in all aspects. Ewha conferred 13 honorary doctorates and 14 awards to those who had made significant contributions to society. Several special events were held over five consecutive days and, among them were, a special revival meeting, the 80th anniversary celebration chapel service, and an International Prayer Fellowship Conference. The government issued postage stamps in commemoration of the 80th anniversary of modern education for women in Korea. The *80 Years History of Ewha,* the *80th Anniversary Commemorative Illustrated Book*, and the *Collection of Essays in Celebration of the 80th Anniversary* were published. For the first time, the school set a day for homecoming alumnae. Ewha graduates from all walks of life gathered to celebrate the school's remarkable history and to select the Alumnae Queen along with the May Queen, a representative of the graduating class.

After the grand 80th anniversary celebration, the Board of Trustees proposed a comprehensive ten-year development plan to transform Ewha into a premier academic research institution. For the first phase (1967-1976) of the plan, a fund-raising campaign was conducted to raise 10 million dollars respectively, from within Korea and from abroad. In Korea, alumnae associations were formed in different regions and workplaces to raise money for the development of their *alma mater*. President Kim Okgill, Chairperson Helen Kim, and staff members of the alumnae association went on provincial tours to organize branch associations across the nation and to enlist all alumnae as members of the Ten-year Development Supporters' Association.

For the overseas fund-raising, Chairperson Helen Kim visited the United States in February 1967. She met her Christian friends and Ewha alumnae in person to explain the development plans and to seek their supports. Peggy Billings was appointed as head of the Ten-year Development Plan Supporters' Association in America. The International Foundation for Ewha Womans University, Inc. was established with the full support of the

American Methodist Church. On April 15, 1970, under the supervision of Peggy Billings, the foundation held its inaugural meeting. In March 1971, the Ewha Womans University Cooperating Board in North America, which was a part of the Missionary Society of the American Methodist Church, merged with the International Foundation for Ewha Womans University, Inc. in an effort to unify the funding campaigns. The Board thus was upgraded to an entity completely independent from the Missionary Society of America.

The successive chairpersons of the Foundation were Betty Mitchell (1971-1978), Kathryne Sears (1979-1980), Mamie Lee Finger (1981-1986), Susan Rubby Lamb (1987-1988), Julia Wilke (1989-1995), and Susanne L. Stevens (1996-). The International Foundation holds its annual general meetings and fund-raising dinners on the first Friday and Saturday of November in major cities in North America, where many Ewha alumnae live.

On February 5, 1970, Professor Helen Kim passed away. She had dedicated all her remaining energy to provide a strong economic foundation for Ewha's development. *The New York Times* reported her death as follows:

"Internationally known Christian Educator, Diplomat, Founder of Ewha Y.W.C.A. First Feminist in Korea, etc. suffering from arteriosclerosis, passed away on Feb 10 at home in Seoul."

"The Experimental University" and the Move toward Internationalization

Korean universities were increasingly restricted in their autonomies and academic freedom in the 1960s under the military dictatorship, and in the 1970s under the authoritarian government structure, fast-paced

5. The Period of Growth (1961-1979)

industrialization, and rigid militaristic culture that pervaded our society.

However, even under these unfavorable circumstances, Ewha was able to transform and actively respond to the age of internationalization. The foundational spirit of Ewha was aimed at restoring the right of women to lead decent lives and promoting the development of human society as a whole. It was now time for Ewha to expand this ideal to the world. Thus Ewha undertook new tasks: first, to hold international symposia and promote international academic exchanges while broadening its outlook; and, second, to identify ways to further promote academic research and establish an academic tradition.

As part of this new endeavor, the University hosted numerous international conferences, such as the First General Meeting of Christian Women's Universities of Asia which was held at Ewha in May 1972. Presidents of 9 universities from 6 countries attended the conference and carried on in-depth discussions on "The Future of Christian Higher Education for Women." At this conference, Professor Chung Ii-sook (Dept. of Christian Studies) presented a paper on "The role of Asian Women's Christian Education." In the paper, she pointed out that the Asian region currently faces three main structural conficts: the conflict between mind and matter, the conflict between tradition and modernity, and the conflict between idea and science. She followed by saying that the Asia faces the challenge of overcoming the present reality mired in such conflicts, and that the future of Asia will depend on how rationally and effectively the issue is addressed.

The other task was institutional restructuring aimed at strengthening the academic programs of the University. One of such endeavors was "the experimental university" system. The experimental university sought extensive reform not only in the school administration but also in relation to students' credits, professor-student relationship and the curriculum. The plans for the experimental university were in accordance with the University Reform Plan of the Ministry of Education, but Ewha was able to implement the experimental university system faster than other schools, having already adopted it as part of the Ten-year Development Plan.

The freshmen of 1973 were the first class to enter Ewha under the experimental university system. The students were admitted into several general areas of study and were given the opportunity to choose their majors after two years of exploring their fields of interest. Because students were given the time to explore different subjects, they were able to choose what they wanted, which was in effect a significant change. This system also enabled the universities to become more competitive. Experimental universities gave the students the ability to make choices and take the initiative in pursuing their studies. It also challenged the professors, as it made free competition a premise in terms of academics or teaching.

In the end, the experimental university system ended as an experiment, but it raised issues that ultimately brought forth positive changes to higher education and a full-scale reform of the curriculum. Such reforms might appear to be foreseen results of the experiment, but it was, in fact, driven by the self-initiated transformation taking place in the academia in response to changes in society. Leading such reform was pushed by the strong leadership of President Kim Okgill and backed by the Office of Academic Administration and the Liberal Arts Education Committee. The reforms that took place at this time provided the impetus for important changes that provided renewed energy to Ewha.

The history of Ewha was a continued endeavor to promote women's self-realization and self-dedication. Through Ewha, women were able to find their identities and pursue truly fulfilling lives. Ewha's commitment to address women's issues materialized with the introduction of women's studies and establishment of the Korean Women's Institute in 1977. The research projects of the Korean Women's Institute were launched to practice Ewha's educational ideals by promoting women's status the world over and realizing an equal society.

The idea of the "integrated women" proposed by Professor Yoon Hoo Jung (Dept. of Law) at this time combined the theories on women's capacity and social structure. It was a more integrated approach that raised the level of discourse on women's issue which had started from the concept of women's education and progressed to equal rights and the super-woman syndrome.

The 1970s and 1980s were tainted by various conflicts in the Korean society. The academia was the center of the strongest resistance against authoritarianism and military dictatorship. Ewha was not an exception. Ewha never abandoned its Christian values, its idea of women's liberation and its dream to contribute to the nation. In this context, Ewha was even more active than other universities. The students' thirst for democracy and social justice were expressed through demonstrations, student debates, special lectures and drama performances.

Ewha's yearning for democracy and justice was best manifested by the vigil prayer strike that took place in the Welch-Ryang Auditorium with the participation of about 4,000 students and President Kim Okgill on November 28, 1973. President Kim always prayed: "Thank you, Lord, for giving us a country deserving your love and for the duty that you have entrusted in us to look after it." These words were expressive of President Kim Okgill's cherished belief in a democratic society based on the free participation of citizens.

Ewha Womans University reached its 90th year in May 1976. It had been 90 years since Ewha had been founded with the mission to raise the quality of human lives in Korean society through the liberation of women. The 90th year was more than a simple occasion for celebration. Ewha had to retake stock of the meaning and value of its existence and to reflect on its commitment to move ahead of the times. The 90th anniversary celebration was held on the morning of May 31. To commemorate the event, special seminars, the Pageant of the May Queen and festivals and special lectures were held. A cornerstone was also laid for the new building of the College of Home Economics.

In her commemorative speech, President Kim Ogkill said, "As Ewha marks its 90th year, it continues to have a clear vision of the future and strives to make the next leap forward. Water that does not flow will rot. We must try, night and day, to continue to flow so that one day we reach the vast ocean." The words clearly stated the will for continuous progress and Ewha's renewed commitment.

Ewha's determination to become a more international institution became stronger. Consequently, as a measure for regular exchanges of academic information, students and professors, faculty exchange programs, the International Summer School and the Graduate School Credit Exchange Programs were initiated. Ewha reached an agreement with Western Michigan University in the U.S. to establish a faculty exchange program, starting in the fall semester of 1972. The International Summer School in Asian Studies was established to provide opportunities for foreign students to study and learn about Korean history and culture. The program further developed and in 1977, the "Kansas at Ewha Program" was jointly established by Kansas University and Ewha. The program offered the foreign students a total of 32 credits of Ewha summer courses related to Korean and Asian studies.

Ewha Old and New : 110 Years of History (1886-1996)

VI

The Take-off Period (1979-1990) :
Reaping the Fruits of 100 Years

6. The Take-off Period (1979-1990) : Reaping the Fruits of 100 Years

Dr. Chung Ii-Sook, the 9th President (1979-1990)

She was steadily working for achieving the vision of the Ewha, "a center of earning and a research-focused university". Passing the 100th anniversary the founding, Ewha developed once again and settled down to the secondary century in spite of politically tumultuous period.

Ewha Old and New : 110 Years of History (1886-1996)

Expanded Campus in 1981

With the implementation of the graduate quota system that limits the number of graduates in return for allowing a larger number of new enrolled students, the size of the campus was doubled to accommodate some 20,000 Ewhaians.

The 100th Anniversary of Ewha (1986)

The 100th anniversary was held under the catch phrase, "One Hundred Years of Dreams, Fulfillment, and Joy."

6. The Take-off Period (1979-1990) : Reaping the Fruits of 100 Years

Ewha Centennial Library (1984)

This is the best university library in Korea. Students can even search for all materials online, and the library's 1,180,000 volumes are managed by a fully computerized system.

June 10 Democracy Movement

Ewhaians enthusiastically participated in the pro-democracy movement that swept the country in June 1987, leading to Korea's first direct presidential election.

Ewha Old and New : 110 Years of History (1886-1996)

Actively Participation in Rural Community

Ewhaians of the 1980s actively participated in rural community service during the planting season in the spring and the harvest season in the fall to provide a helping hand to farmers. This photo shows a scene of rural community service in the fall of 1988.

Establishment of Ewha Womans University Archives (1989)

The Archives were established in October 1989 to research the history of Ewha and arrange and preserve materials and data. This photo shows Prof. Maynor's class at Ewha College in the 1930s represented in a diorama and displayed in the Ewha archives exhibition, "Leading the World, Creating the Future; Ewha in History" held in 2000. The diorama is on display in the Ewha Archives Exhibition Hall on the second floor of the university museum.

6. The Take-off Period (1979-1990) :
Reaping the Fruits of 100 Years

The Great Stride Forward

In September of 1979, President Kim Okgill, who had led Ewha for 18 years, ended her term these final words: "Ewha has entered an era that requires new changes and developments. Therefore, for Ewha's development, it is time for a younger, more talented person with a greater ability to serve as president." President Kim Okgill's surprising decision was widely regarded as exceptionally valiant and exemplary in the power-oriented and undemocratic society.

The newly elected 9th President of Ewha, Chung Ii-sook graduated from the English Language and Literature of Ewha Womans University and received her Ph. D. in the Education of Religion at the Graduate School of Northwestern University in the U.S. She was a pioneer of women's studies in Korea and had served at Ewha for over 20 years. She had always emphasized the need to live the life of a Christian intellectual in which Christian ideals are practiced.

In her inaugural speech delivered on September 1, 1979, President Chung discussed in detail the important aspects of Ewha history. She also defined the duty and values demanded of the university at that particular historical moment. Her speech conveyed a new direction for Korean universities in the 1980s, and came as a wake-up call to universities across the nation. She summarized the essence of Ewha's ideals as "Ewha intellect" which can only be realized when one leads a life of practicing one's knowledge. Ewhaians should become "historical mothers" who can heal the Korean people's wounds by combining their intelligence and love for others, she said.

President Chung reassessed the tasks facing Ewha. Firstly, it is important for Ewha to focus on character education based on Christian values. Secondly, Ewha needs to further its growth as an institution of higher learning and advanced research. Thirdly, Ewha needs to produce qualified women leaders equipped with both theory and practical skills. Fourthly, as an educational institution, Ewha must fulfill its role of enabling the betterment of women's lives and enhancing their consciousness and capacity. Fifthly, Ewha should not limit the period of learning for its students, but instead provide opportunities for life-long learning. Sixthly, Ewha must realign its administration system as well as its regulations with current times and make the system more efficient, effective and relevant. Seventhly, in order to implement the aforementioned six tasks, Ewha must strive to become financially efficient and to expand its facilities and upgrade its infrastructure based on year-by-year planning.

President Chung Ii-sook also presented the future direction for Ewha as she closed her remarks. "Ewha Womans University is an institution that realizes the ideal woman - a woman with ability, intelligence and compassion. Its role in our people's history should be a mother who nurtures and heals those in need, and also a friend who shares the joys and pains of the people." The inauguration address that President Chung delivered was significant as it not only presented the moral goals of Ewha but also the future direction for Korean universities.

Soon after these words were spoken, the nation underwent great political turmoil. On October 26, 1979, President Park Chung-hee was assassinated, and the long-standing military dictatorial rule collapsed. Korea experienced a period of serious social upheaval amid a power vacuum. Universities were also drawn into the maelstrom of violent political unrest. Student demonstrators began to fill the streets of Seoul, bonded by the ardent desire for democracy that characterized the spring of 1980. On May 17, 1980, the government declared emergency martial law throughout the nation, and the nation was going into another period of military rule.

The 1980s was a decade of crisis and formidable changes. The times demanded the new set of responses from Ewha. First, Ewha faced the challenge of maintaining its original Christian values. Second, Ewha had to deal actively with the changing situation to exert a powerful and positive influence on society. Third, Ewha had developed into an intellectual body of elite women in Korea, but social changes demanded that Ewha transforms itself into a more inclusive university. Fourth, Ewha had to remain competitive in a society where both men and women could demonstrate their talents on an equal footing to improve society. Thus, Ewha in the 1980s had to both maintain traditional values and ideas and develop new ones in educating capable young Ewhaians. Indeed, the changing times were asking Ewha to be born again.

The military regime of Gen. Jeon Doo-hwan unilaterally enforced the graduate quota system on universities as of July 30, 1980. The system required universities to admit 130% of the usual freshman enrollment and to fail 30% of the students depending on their academic standing after four years of competition with their peers. As the new system was implemented, the number of students at Ewha increased from 10,000 to 20,000. In the face of this sudden increase, Ewha's ideas and Christian traditions came to be challenged. The university was no longer a place for scholarly pursuit, but a jungle of intense competition. Students were graded on a sliding scale, academic probations were issued, and many students took voluntary leave for fear of dismissal.

Introducing Modern Management for a Research-focused University

President Chung Ii-sook drew up a set of concrete plans to be executed during her term. It was a blueprint to enhance the academic capacity of the school and produce women leaders of faith, competency and historical consciousness. The key words that President Chung emphasized were a "center of learning and research-focused university."

Ewha's pursuit of becoming a research-focused university was focused in two areas. The first was to support the development of specialized institutes to promote research activities of the faculty. The second was to place top priority on academic excellence throughout the school with particular emphasis on graduate students.

Specific measures were taken. Committees were formed to study and review plans. New systems were put in place to upgrade the quality of education and research; support for research was strengthened in order to recruit qualified professors, and scholarships and other incentives were introduced to attract outstanding students.

The student/faculty ratio was improved, and as a result, the size of faculty increased from 330 in 1980 to 424 in 1990. In order to promote academic research, professors were encouraged to participate in research collaboration with major overseas research institutes, and the amount of research grants issued by the school to individual professors was also increased. From 1986, research-focused projects were carried out to promote the outstanding academic achievements. The Ewha Faculty Research Fund was established in 1986 in order to support the professors in publishing research work and academic papers, and also to support the activities for those in the arts and performance area.

Another task was to enhance the capacity of research centers in the university. First, the existing centers were reviewed, and those with overlapping functions were consolidated, while new ones were created to fill any gaps. The system was changed so that research grants were to be distributed through bodies directly reporting to the President, such as the Korean Cultural Research Institute and the Korean Research Institute for Better Living. New research centers were created in the advanced sciences field, including the Computer Research Center (1983), Research Institute of Basic Science (1985) and Institute of Bioscience (1990).

In addition to supporting these research centers, President Chung Ii-sook introduced the graduate programs for Women's Studies and Korean Studies to strengthen research in these areas. "Not only must Ewha fulfill its role of enabling the betterment of women's lives and enhancing their consciousness and capacity, but also Ewhaians themselves must become self-reliant persons with a sense of individuality, social consciousness, historical awareness, and must fulfill their duties towards the nation and history." Based on this conviction, President Chung established the Department of Women Studies in 1982. The new Department would be playing a leading role and working in tandem with the Korean Women's Institute to create a new tradition in the university. Furthermore, the Graduate School of Industrial Design was established in 1982 to provide professional training both in theory and practice, and to act as an incubator for future women leaders in the field of industrial design.

A Special Scholarship Program was introduced to attract outstanding students, and a new system was put in place to ensure that more than 20% of the students could benefit from scholarships. The number of Teaching Assistants was increased from 1981, so that more graduate students could receive scholarships.

Another essential task required to become a research-focused university was the improvement of the educational quality. President Chung set up the

Committee for General Studies with the aim of increasing the number of general studies courses offered to students in their first year, allowing them to be exposed to a wider variety of subjects before choosing a major in their second year. Many of the general studies courses were designated as prerequisite courses for major studies in order to increase the level of interest in these courses. The required major course credits toward a degree were also increased from 51 to 60, and the number of major courses was also increased.

For Ewha to become a "center of learning and a research-focused university," the administrative structure needed to become more efficient. Computerizing academic and general administration work was first done. Course registration, admission related processes and financial accounting were computerized in sequence, followed by the remaining administrative processes. The 3-year Library Computerization Plan of was drawn up and was implemented from 1988 to 1990. A merit-rating system was introduced to the administrative staff to effectuate a more efficient administrative and personnel management process. All academic administration was centralized to the college Administration Office, so that individual departments could be alleviated of their administrative work load and concentrate on functioning as a communication channel between students and faculty.

Other institutes were created or restructured. The newly created institutes include the Speech and Hearing Center (1981), Graduate School of Industrial Design (1981), Computer Research Center (1983), School of Continuing Education (1984), International Education Institute (1985) and Ewha Womans University Archives (1989). Other organizations were restructured, such as the Ewha Kindergarten and Institute of Language Education.

The establishment of the School of Continuing Education was a realization of a vision that President Chung had from the early days of her term in office. President Chung's founding philosophy was that Ewha should be a learning community for all women, and thus a place for life-long learning where the educational opportunities are not confined to a certain period but provided throughout life whenever necessary.

The Ewha Womans University Archives is an organization with the mission of diligently preserving, researching and compiling documents and materials related to the long history of Ewha. It was established to function as a focal point serving to facilitate the transmission and inheritance of Ewha's history, tradition and ideals, and to help establish a common identity among Ewhaians. Ewha Womans University Archives was the first university archive to build an exhibition hall for the history of Ewha and thus serves as a model in many ways.

Such reforms would not have been possible without the great effort made by President Chung to improve the financial state of the university. At the time President Chung came into office, Ewha's financial state was in a dire situation. One of the biggest achievements of President Chung was to build a sound financial base for Ewha by introducing modern management techniques, and actively raising funds through sponsorships, donations and loans. Once financial soundness was secured, plans went ahead to expand the educational facilities with new buildings that were spatially efficient and architecturally beautiful. The landscape of the campus was also altered to be more beautiful. These accomplishments that took place during President Chung's term made everyone feel proud to be an Ewhaian.

When the graduate quota system was enforced in 1980, the number of students grew dramatically and resulted in a chronic shortage of space on campus. The long-term plan drawn out by President Chung included the construction of a new lecture building (Ewha-Posco Building), a faculty center, individual college buildings and a second Ewha hospital. She also made plans for the expansion of the student dormitory and the university hospital in Tongdaemun, as well as plans for a second campus site - all of which she pursued with great passion. Consequently, during President Chung's term, the Business Administration Building (1982), Ewha Centennial Library (1984), Science Building (1984), Kosa-ri Retreat Center (1985), Law and Political Science Building (1986), Ah-ryoung Dang (Home Management House, 1986), Ewha Kindergarten (1986) and Ewha Centennial Museum (1989) were newly constructed. Meanwhile, the Ceramic Research Institute, Alumnae Building and Emma Hall (Education Hall) were expanded.

The Ewha Centennial Library was completed in May 1984, in commemoration of the school's 100th anniversary which was two years away. The entire Ewha family — professors, staff and alumnae — along with friends of Ewha made donations to fund the construction. The library has 4,000 seats and over 1 million volumes of book and is the first library in Korea to run an open access system throughout the entire facility. Not only is the library the largest in the country, but is also most technologically advanced, with a computer lab and a web-based cataloging system that can be accessed online.

The Science Building A housing the College of Natural Science and the science and math education departments of the College of Education. Building A was completed in 1982, and Building B was completed in 1984. Both buildings are equipped with state-of-the-art equipment and effectively support science education and research.

The Ewha Centennial Museum is the first building on left inside the main gate of Ewha campus. Completed in 1989, the building is shaped in the image of the school symbol, the five-petal pear blossom, and is furnished with the facilities required for the preservation of its collection. Ewha Museum has been at the forefront of museology in Korea for the past 60 years. Its collection includes a Joseon white porcelain which was designated as a national treasure, 11 other national treasures, as well as many other cultural artifacts of Korea.

6. The Take-off Period (1979-1990) : Reaping the Fruits of 100 Years

The construction of the Kosa-ri Retreat Center was completed in 1985. The Center is an off-campus facility located in Yeonpung-myeon, Gwesan-gun of North Chungcheong Province and serves as a venue for many student events, such as student Membership Training. It is also open to Ewha faculty and staff, as well as the local community.

A new wing was added to Ewha Dongdaemun Hospital, and the existing buildings were expanded between 1983 and 1985. In 1983, a new site was acquired in accordance with the plan to build a second university hospital in the Mokdong where a new town was to be developed.

During President Chung's term, it seemed that a new building was going up every day. The campus bustled with construction and was filled with excitement and anticipation. Ewha was full of energy as new sophisticated buildings were constructed and an advanced management system was introduced. It was the time when Ewha made great strides and grew exponentially.

The Centennial : Dreams, Fulfillment and Joy

The centennial of Ewha was a joyful event not only for Ewhaians. It was a momentous milestone in the history of Korea. The 100 years of Ewha marked the 100 years of modern Korea. It was a long journey of liberating women from social exclusion and enabling them to lead humane and dignified lives.

The centennial celebration focused on highlighting the essence of Ewha, and realizing the true ideals of the university. A Centennial Committee was set up to plan and organize Ewha's centennial projects. The main projects were the compilation of The *100 Years History of Ewha*, academic symposia,

117

completion of the Ewha Centennial Library, ground breaking for the construction of the centennial museum, publication of an academic journal, fund-raising for the special lectures and the publication of a series of books on Korean culture and the *Woowol Anthology Volume II* in commemoration of Dr. Helen Kim. Other projects included writing a commemoration song, issuing commemorative stamps, creating a centennial logo and conferring honorary doctorate degrees and awards.

At ten o'clock in the morning of May 31, 1986, the Centennial ceremony was held on Ewha's main ground attended by about 15,000 people filled with excitement and solemnity. In her commemorative address, President Chung Ii-sook said, "Ewha is the realization of God's will that has saved an entire nation. Ewha's 100 years of history was dedicated to advancing the cause of women and bettering their lives, therefore, it is testimony to the great human potential."

The commemorative address emphasized the need for planning a new future and renewing the commitment to carry on the spirit of Ewha.

The first commitment Ewha Womans University will make this day is the commitment to remain on the side of God and truth in ages to come. The second commitment is to be the vanguard of realizing the eternal dream of human emancipation. The third commitment is to play a central role in bringing the forces together for reuniting our divided nation. The fourth commitment to put our energy and passion into becoming a cornerstone for a peaceful world. These four commitments are the answer to the callings of our times, as we enter the second century of Ewha's history. It is what we all aspire to : everyone gathered here at this ceremony and everyone else living in this age and time. Ewha will continue on with its mission of educating and working for human salvation and emancipation. We will answer to any call for

6. The Take-off Period (1979-1990) : Reaping the Fruits of 100 Years

dedication and commit ourselves to the goal of human emancipation.

"One hundred years of dreams, one hundred years of fulfillments, one hundred years of joy. Lord, be forever with Ewha's spirit." When these words of the 100th anniversary commemoration song reverberated in the hearts of all Ewhaians and filled them with emotion. The ceremony was an opportunity to reflect upon the past 100 years with overwhelming gratitude and to envision the next 100 years of Ewha with great expectations.

The First 100 Years and Renewed Commitment for Growth

In 1987, President Chung embarked upon a plan to formulate a new "Ewha Development Master Plan." 1987 was a significant point in time; the first 100 years were now behind, and Ewha was opening a new chapter in its history. In September 1986, President Chung had already launched the Ewha Development Task Force Committee at the university level and corresponding committees at the individual college level.

The Ewha Development Master Plan had a two-tiered structure, in which individual colleges would prepare respective development proposals while a central comprehensive development plan was drawn up at the university level. For over three years, these committees conducted wide-ranging and in-depth research on Ewha's educational direction and vision for the future. As a result of such researches, the Ewha Development Master Plan was finally completed. It can be summarized as follows: improvement of the effectiveness and efficiency of the curriculum; expansion of the student body and corresponding development of the academic system; improvement of administration functions; enlargement of faculty; better research environment for faculty; improvement of student administrations; and improvement of educational and research facilities. These indicate the main directions for Ewha to take in its second century.

President Chung set a new course by placing emphasis on areas where women were underrepresented, such as business, economy, science, engineering, architecture, as well as advanced sciences. In addition, a new set of educational objective were established: to promote reconciliation and peace based on Christian values and disseminate the message in a world fraught with disparity and conflict; to provide creative and selfless services to ethnic minorities and underprivileged people in the third world; and to produce women leaders capable of contributing to world peace.

Ewha worked tirelessly for the past 100 years in the single minded pursuit of its goals : spreading the Christian Good News while educating and nurturing women talents. On top of these traditional values, President Chung reestablished the educational goals for Ewha's second century, and presented the direction for its development with the belief that, "The future of society is dictated by the quality of higher education, and education will determine the nation's international standing." President Chung Ii-sook's visionary insight played a decisive role and provided the foundation for the "Ewha 21st Century Development Plan."

Ewha Old and New : 110 Years of History (1886-1996)

VII

Ewha - On the Road to Becoming a World-Renowned University in the 21st Century (1990-1996)

7. Ewha - On the Road to Becoming a World-Renowned University in the 21st Century (1990-1996)

Dr. Yoon Hoo Jung, the 10th President (1990-1996)

President Yoon, the first elected in direct election, drew up and implemented the "Ewha 21st Century Development Plan", a set of guidelines for Ewha's future education to make Ewha a world-renowned university.

Opening of Mokdong Hospital (1993)

Ewha's university hospital, which boasts a history of 117 years, has grown into two huge university hospitals, each equipped with the most advanced facilities and highly-trained medical teams.

Ewha Ranked First in the Nationwide University Evaluation (1995)

Ewha's efforts to improve the quality of its education have been recognized objectively on many occasions. It was selected as a model school of educational reform, and its graduate school was qualified for national support for the training of international professionals. When the results of the evaluations were announced, Ewha was ranked first among all of the universities in the country.

7. Ewha - On the Road to Becoming a World-Renowned University in the 21st Century (1990-1996)

World's First Women's College of Engineering (1996)

To meet the demands of industry for high-quality female engineers, Ewha established the world's first women's college of engineering in 1996. Asan Hall (Engineering Building), a five-story engineering building with a basement floor, was constructed in July 1996 and has a total floor space of 9,900m². It boasts a wide range of sophisticated facilities and has produced numerous female engineers. The college introduced the system of post-selection of majors in 1999, and it now has some 1,000 undergraduates and 250 graduate students.

Signing Ceremony for an Academic Exchange Agreement with Beijing University in China (1996)

Ewha Old and New : 110 Years of History (1886-1996)

The Promotion of Bachelor's Degree Holders as Transfer Students, Dual Majors have allowed students more opportunities to experience a wider range of academic fields rather than a single discipline.

The Beautiful World by Ewhaian - the Social Service March
Ewhaians take a walk through campus with physically challenged children.

7. Ewha - On the Road to Becoming a World-Renowned University in the 21st Century (1990-1996)

Ewha's Vision and 100 Challenges

Yoon Hoo Jung was inaugurated the 10th president of Ewha Womans University in August 1990 when Chung Ii-sook's term was expired. Yoon, elected with an overwhelming majority in the first direct election involving the whole faculty, majored in law at Ewha and gained her doctoral degree in law (S.J.D.) at Northwestern University, which is a difficult degree for foreign students to obtain. She has played a central role not only in Korea's legal and education circles but also in the field of women's studies.

As the inaugural chairperson of the Korean Association of Women's Studies, Yoon took an early interest in the betterment of women's lives and has promoted the "integrated woman" as the most ideal and complete image of woman. The "integrated woman" is a woman who transcends gender distinctions with respect to consciousness, values, abilities and roles; a woman who can work with and complement men as equal partner ; and a woman who can adapt to and proactively participate in politics and history.

The history of Ewha was a long process of nurturing such women in the male-dominated and patriarchal society of Korea. Furthermore, Ewha will continue to uphold and advance the idea of the integrated woman. While stating that Ewha must continue to emphasize the role of women as "mothers of the nation" who nurture and heal the wounds of the people, Yoon also presented a long-term vision for the school, presaging the age of globalization and information.

The 1990s was a period of great change, such as people have never before experienced. The age of internationalization, globalization, and regionalization and a world without borders had arrived, and science and technology had become highly advanced and information-based.

At a time that called for great change in human society to meet the 21st century, in September 1990 Yoon established a grand, future-oriented plan for Ewha and formed the 20-member University Development Planning Committee (chairperson: Eung-yeon Hwang) which was put in charge of drawing up wide-ranging reform plans.

A sabbatical system was established giving professors who had served more than seven years at Ewha the opportunity to take a year off to concentrate on research. Also, a professor emeritus system was introduced to honor professors who served for more than 20 years at Ewha and who have made outstanding academic achievements during that time.

In addition, an accomplished scholarship system was established in order to invite distinguished senior professors to teach at Ewha. In May 1991, U.N. Mazur from Moscow University and In-ho Lee from Seoul National University became the first professors to lecture at Ewha under this system. Other professors invited through this program, designed to bring eminent scholars from inside and outside Korea to teach at Ewha and in this way promote research and expose students to wider scholarship, including Halina Ogarek Czoj from Warsaw University, Mark Klino Taylor from Princeton University, and Ildiko Hrubos from Budapest University. From 1994, the invitation of endowed professors has been carried out on a semester basis.

Those taking part in this program have all been leaders in Korean society with strong academic backgrounds and include Soon Cho, former deputy

7. Ewha - On the Road to Becoming a World-Renowned University in the 21st Century (1990-1996)

prime minister; Woo-dong Park, former justice of the Supreme Court; Ou-ryung Lee, former Minister of Culture and Sports; and Kyung-shik Kang, particle physicist. In March 1994, the graduate school held the "Memorial Lecture for Helen Kim" and invited the world-famous microbiologist Dr. Kyoung-joo Kwon.

Meanwhile, economic liberalization and globalization called for opening in the education and cultural sectors as well, and increasing the competitiveness of universities became an important issue. The tide of openness and competition impelled Ewha also to reform and change in new ways.

Having great insight into the development of future society, Yoon realized that the 21st century would be one of epochal change and accordingly created the basic framework for Ewha's development by presenting Ewha's vision and goal — Ewha as "a world-renowned university" — and the areas to be emphasized toward achieving this goal — "specialization", "information technology", "globalization", "science", and "welfare".

In order to build on this basic concept and put it into action, in March 1992, the aforementioned University Development Planning Committee was reorganized and renamed the University Development Committee (chairperson: Eung-yeon Hwang). The committee was divided into five sub-committees and assigned five specific tasks to be studied : 1) Ewha in the future, 2) restructuring the colleges and departments, 3) establishment of a College of Engineering, 4) establishment of professional graduate schools, and 5) construction of new buildings and expansion of existing buildings. The findings of their studies were examined and discussed in numerous school and faculty meetings to form consensus among all Ewha staff.

At the same time the Reorganization Preparatory Committee was formed(chairperson : Byeong-wook Choi). This committee created the basic framework for reorganization of the school and administration, which has been in progress since March 1993 to the present.

On August 18, 1993, President Yoon held a press conference where she officially announced that specialization, information technology, globalization, science and welfare were the areas Ewha would focus on in its development plans, and also announced a grand development plan for a new beginning for Ewha, the details of which included construction of a second campus, establishment of a College of Engineering, and a 100-billion-won fund raising campaign.

While implementing the plan, in October 1993 President Yoon reformed existing committees to create the Ewha 21st Century Development Planning Committee (47-member chairperson, Seok-jun Kim) and established a comprehensive and detailed plan for development of the school. Research was carried out by 10 sub-committees in ten areas: 1) globalization of Ewha education, 2) establishment of the Ewha Academy and Academy of Sciences, 3) restructuring the academic system along with the establishment of new organizations and expansion of existing ones, 4) rationalization of university administration, 5) strengthening unity in the Ewha community, 6) master plan for the campus, 7) increasing the capacity of the faculty, 8) improving the quality of education, 9) securing educational finances and making use of the Eunji-ri site, and 10) overall plan. From their findings "100 challenges" were set and these have been put into action since 1994, marking a turning point in the development of the school. In May 1994, the Ewha 21st Century Development Patrons Committee (chairperson: Dr. Geun-mo Chung) was established to secure funding for the school.

Meanwhile, to strengthen the school and increase quality of education, revision of the school curriculum began in March 1992 and the new curriculum -reduction in the number of required subjects, establishment of integrated courses, and emphasis on women's studies subjects- was put into effect in March 1994, bringing many changes to fit the changing times.

Establishment of linked undergraduate and graduate courses also began at this time.

Ewha in its Second Century : On the Road to Globalization

On May 28, 1994, a great celebration was held for Ewha's 108th anniversary, and a new beginning for the school in preparation for the 21st century was proclaimed. In a ceremony attended by 4,000 people including school faculty and staff, students, alumnae and representatives from society, President Yoon announced Ewha's development plans for the 21st century, the "100 challenges", and Ewha's vision for the 21st century. Yoon proclaimed the goal to turn Ewha from a leading Korean university into a world-renowned university, and affirmed the commitment of the Ewha community to realize this goal. She then presented the "100 challenges" for achieving Ewha's goals of educating top women leaders and becoming a research-focused university. This was the roadmap for Ewha's endeavor to become a worldrenowned university.

For the first time in Ewha's history, spouses of alumnae were invited to the ceremony, and the event was attended by over 400 men who were prominent leaders of the Korean society.

In the meantime, *The 100 Years History of Ewha* and *The 100 years of Ewha Historical Documents and Artifacts*: were published after many years of preparation, marking another milestone in the school history. Rather than being a simple history of Ewha, *The 100 Years History of Ewha* is the story of Ewha intertwined with the history of modern Korea, modern Korean women, and modern Korean education. It is no exaggeration to say that the history of Ewha is an integral part of the modern history of Korea. The publication of *The 100 Years History of Ewha* is recognized as a historical event in the Korean society. Ewha was taking looking back at the past century and proclaiming its plans and visions for the next century.

As stated by President Yoon, the focus of Ewha's educations reform was placed on globalization, information technology, and science, and consisted of reforms in the academic system as well as its administration. The development plan designed to turn Ewha into a "center of learning and a research-focused university" was sub-divided into seven areas: educational reform, strengthening research, community service, unity as a learning community, administrative efficiency, better use of environment and space, and securing of funding.

As an institutional measure to overcome the traditionally closed academic system and to expose students to a wider academic world, Ewha started to accept bachelor's degree holders as transfer students, and dual majors were allowed from the second semester of 1994. In the first semester of 1996, a new system was introduced and first implemented in the Colleges of Libral Arts, Social Science, Natural Sciences, Business Administration, Pharmacy, and Home Science & Management. Unlike the traditional norm, this system admitted new students into several general areas of study and allowed them to spend the first year exploring a wide range of subjects before choosing major in the second year. By doing so, students exposed to a wider range of choices. Along with this new system, the curriculum was greatly revised so that the number of credits required for graduation and minimum credits for each major was reduced. In addition, the number of books in the library collection reached one million.

To keep step with the age of globalization, the International Education Institute, Ewha's channel of international education exchange, was expanded. The sister university program which had been pursued with foreign universities since 1985 resulted in sister relationships with 49 schools in 10 countries, including 28 schools in the United States and other Western countries, as well as Beijing University in China, and Warsaw University in Poland. Active exchange of students and professors is taking place and the annual International Co-Ed Summer School held during summer vacation gives the children of Koreans living around the world the opportunity to live in and experience their home country.

President Yoon particularly emphasized science and technology as a field that women should make inroads into and concentrated efforts on developing the school's capacity in the field of natural sciences. As a result of the endeavors to establish a College of Engineering and achievements in the basic sciences, the Department of Environmental Science was founded in 1992, followed by the Department of Information Electronics Engineering and the Department of Architecture in 1994. In 1996 Ewha finally received approval to establish a College of Engineering from the Ministry of Education, marking a great achievement in women's education.

The completion of the Engineering Building, which provides a state-of-the-art learning environment, is particularly meaningful considering that Ewha's College of Engineering is the first in the world to be established in a women's university. Ewha thus prepared the launch pad for its entry into the 21st century, the age of women and the age of science, and for its progress toward becoming a world-renowned university.

A joint university-research complex program was established with the Korea Institute of Science and Technology (K.I.S.T.) in December 1994 and with Pohang University of Science and Technology in February 1995, marking the start of academic exchange and joint research with the country's foremost research institutions in the field of natural sciences and engineering. Such cooperation with other organizations was instrumental and helped to overcome the limitations of a women's university.

To increase the competitiveness of women as professionals in the workforce, the Ewha Institute for Professional Certification was established in 1995 to operate certificate programs in business administration, computer skills, and languages. In order to produce broadcasting professionals, the Educational Multimedia Center opened the Ewha Broadcasting Academy (27.2.1995) and offered script writing and broadcast announcer courses.

As academic research is the main function of a university, President Yoon set as a priority the invitation of distinguished professors and expansion of the research capacity of existing faculty. An open recruitment system was introduced for the first time, and 320 qualified members were added to the faculty between 1991 and 1996.

As of the end of 1996, there were 649 full-time professors, which fulfilled the legal requirement by 95 percent (99 percent if medical clinical staffs are included) and improved the student faculty ratio to 24:1. And in 1994, Ewha became the first university in Korea to introduce the students' course evaluation system.

In the first semester of 1995, 30 native speakers were hired as full-time lecturers, enabling more English-language lectures, smaller foreign language classes, use of OHP, and field trips for students. Also, for realistic practical experience the Ewha color broadcasting station was opened (24.3.1995).

Concrete adjustments were made to the organization of the University to reflect such changes, and Ewha's organization was broadly categorized into research-focused colleges, professional education colleges, and music, arts & sports colleges (22.8.1995). The integration of the College of Liberal Arts with the College of Law, a long-time goal of Ewha, was carried out and the independent Colleges of Liberal Arts, Social Sciences, Law and Business Administration were newly established (Feb. 1996) to enhance the academic capacity of colleges in a more effective manner. From February 1995, Ewha also introduced more flexibility in academic administration and selected areas of "specialization" in which Ewha would foster its core competence.

7. Ewha - On the Road to Becoming a World-Renowned University in the 21st Century (1990-1996)

Ewha, as the birthplace and the center of women's studies in Korea, has produced many teachers of women's studies who are now active in universities across the country. In March 1991, doctoral degree programs were established in the Department of Women's Studies and the Department of Computer Science. By offering an increased number of women's studies courses, and by enhancing the role of the women researchers in this field, Ewha assumed the role as a center of women's studies in the Asian region.

Much energy was devoted into the fields of information technology and biotechnology, with the aim of cultivating women leaders who could fully demonstrate women's capabilities in the age of science in the 21st century. Toward that end, the Institute of Bioscience (1990) was expanded and renamed the Research Institute of Basic Sciences (1993). And also several new institutes were established including the Ewha Institute for Women's Theological Studies (1993), the Ewha Legal Science Institute, the Medical Research Center, the Human Ecology Environmental Institute (1995), the Institute for International Trade and Cooperation, the Research Institute of Natural History, the Music Institute of Ewha Womans University, and the Asian Center for Women's Studies (1995). Work also began on establishing the Ewha Color Design Institute (1994-95).

In addition, the Korean Women's Institute was expanded in December 1994 which, along with the Asian Center for Women's Studies, has led specialization of women's studies, policy making, and women's studies education, both inside and outside of Korea. In March 1992, the Korean Women's Institute was commissioned with the task of conducting comparative studies on North Korean women and Korean-Chinese women and strengthening academic exchange. Significant , progress has been made so far in both areas. The institute began a project in second semester 1993 to make profile cards of Ewha graduates (simple history of Ewha graduates, and vocational statistics), the first phase of which has been completed.

Under the leadership of the Public Relations Office at the University Office of Planning and Coordination, the monthly publication *Ewha Sosik* (*Ewha News*) was launched on August 1, 1993. Also, the school completed the 1st phase management evaluation of each organization within the school (1.12.93 to 28.2.94).

All the while, graduate schools continued to step up efforts to develop into research-focused institutions. The enrollment capacity for graduate schools was increased as well as the number of available courses, while efforts were focused on establishing specialized and professional graduate schools. The Graduate School of Social Welfare was established in 1993, and the Graduate School of Information Science and the Women's Supreme Leadership Course in 1995. These specialized graduate schools offer evening courses in order to provide re-education opportunities to women professionals already in the workforce.

Ewha also made further reforms toward the goal of becoming a research-focused university. In 1995, Ewha applied to the Ministry of Education for approval to establish the Graduate School of Translation and Interpretation, the Graduate School of International Studies, the Graduate School of Theology, the Graduate School of Clinical Health Sciences, the Graduate School of Law, and the Graduate School of Policy Sciences. The Graduate School of Translation and Interpretation and the Graduate School of International Studies were opened in 1997, and the Graduate School of Theology and the Graduate School of Policy Sciences were established in 1998.

While enhancing the climate for academic research, Ewha also concentrated its efforts on community service. In September 1993 a new university hospital was opened in Mokdong and the College of Medicine moved off campus to the medical research building next to the new hospital. The existing Dongdaemun Hospital and the new Mokdong Hospital have

500 and 600 beds, respectively, and offer specialized treatment in 20 medical fields to local residents. Every year, during the winter holidays, the College of Medicine opens the Ewha Medical Camp in Katmandu, Nepal, and offers medical services in areas where medical facilities are inadequate.

More than ever before, Ewha greatly expanded the channel for direct service to the local community through such means as expansion and enhancement of programs offered by the School of Continuing Education, establishment of the Graduate School of Social Welfare, expansion of the role of the Community Welfare Center, and recognition of volunteer work for academic credits.

At this time, the School of Continuing Education achieved noticeable growth. The curriculum was reorganized in 1994 and four new courses were created — professional studies, general studies, general studies for career women, and special activities. And new courses were continuously added, including life-long learning courses, re-education courses, specialized professional training courses, and vocational training courses. The courses are taken by 1,600 students every semester allowing the School of Continuing Education to contribute to the education of women professionals in all fields of society. In addition, Ewha is serving the local community through the Institute of Language Education, the University Museum, and the Natural History Museum which have all been expanded to offer diverse public education programs.

Significant reforms took place in the administrative area to enhance efficiency and to build an educational environment befitting the high-tech information society. First, the Office of Admissions and the Office of University Relations and Development were created in 1994. This was followed by , the completion of the campus-wide computer network in 1995, which dramatically increased the efficiency in handling administrative and academic affairs.

The campus network project was launched in 1991 when the Network Development Committee was formed, and after three years of detailed research and analysis, the ground was broken for construction of an advanced campus-wide network in 1994. Fiber optic cables were laid connecting all departments and organizations in the school as well as off-campus sites such as the Dongdaemun Hospital and Mokdong Hospital. In the autumn of 1995, Ewha-Net and the Ewha Integrated Information System (E.T.I.S.) went into full operation.

The network enabled computerized processing of academic administration, and all students and staff of Ewha were issued IDs for accessing the network from anywhere on campus. Students were able to access the library's online catalogue system, sign up for courses online, and also view Internet video lectures. Ewha also signed an agreement with computer companies Haansoft and Microsoft to be provided with educational software.

In the 1990s, great changes took place on campus. The gymnasium was expanded (17.6.91) and many new buildings were erected including the Humanities Hall (faculty building) (2.12.92), Mokdong Hospital and Medical Research Institute (9.9.93), the new Pharmaceutical Science Building (30.6.94), the College of Medicine's Sudong-myeon Community Health Center (7.6.95), and Asan Hall (Engineering Building, 23.7.96). Hanisol Building (foundation building, (6.12.95) and the Ewha Haktang Chungjeong Building (14.3.96) were also completed.

In addition, the electronic switching equipment was replaced and fax equipments installed (April, 1991), and the Ewha campus network and the development of the Ewha Integrated Information System (E.T.I.S.) were completed (30.11.95). Construction began on new buildings such as the Museum of Natural History (30.6.94), the Ewha-Samsung Culture Center (2.6.95), the Student Union Building (19.3.96), the Ewha-SK Telecom Center

(23.8.96), and Hanwoori Hall (new dormitory) and the International Hall (29.8.96).

The Welch-Ryang Auditorium was renovated and repaired for the first time since it was built in 1956, and major repair and maintenance work was carried out on the Hakkwan, Case Hall (the Graduate School Building), the Appenzeller Hall, the Jinsunmi Hall, the Fine Arts Building, and the old Music Building. In a university-wide faculty meeting in February 1996, a plan was announced to build an intelligent building for the social sciences on the old dormitory site, to be later named the Ewha-POSCO Building, and a new University Church, and extensions and renovations were carried out on the Science Center Building.

In 1995, Ewha celebrated its 109th founding anniversary and the 60th anniversary of relocating to the Sinchon campus. In the ceremony for 60th anniversary of the Sinchon campus, the restored Appenzeller sundial was unveiled. Sixty years ago, the Shinchon campus had only four buildings and 350 students. Now the campus has 40 buildings and 20,000 students.

Furthermore, President Yoon Hoo Jung and foundation Chairperson Chung Ii-sook took special interest in the railway-covering project Ewha Bridge. Much work went into persuading the relevant administrative authorities, and no effort was spared in order to preserve the campus environment and secure more classroom space. As a result, in 2001 the groundbreaking ceremony for the Ewha Bridge railway-covering project was held.

At the 109th Ewha anniversary ceremony in 1995, the first "Proud Ewha Alumna Award" ceremony was given out. The first honorees were former first lady Myung-soon Sohn, Dr. Tae-yeong Lee, Korea's first woman lawyer who fought to revise the family law and increased women's rights and was a leader in the democratization movement; Dr. Kyoung-joo Kwon, an international authority on medical mycology and head of the molecular microbiology section of U.S. National Institutes of Health; and Won-sook Lee, mother of the famous Chung trio : Myung-wha Chung, Kyung-wha Chung and Myung-whun Chung.

In subsequent years, the Proud Ewha Alumna Award has been given to such people as Dr. Emma Kim who founded the college of education at Ewha, the first in a private university in Korea; Sin-ae Jeon who fought to raise the status of minorities in the United States as labor Secretary of the state of Illinois; Dr. Gil-jae Lim, the first Asian to gain a license to provide medical service in New York and dedicated member of the Ewha International Foundation; Hyo-jae Lee who has worked hard to bring the military sexual slavery issued by Japan to international attention; and Im-sun Kim who has devoted her life to work for the needy and underprivileged in Korean society, starting with her work with the Korean War orphans.

In addition, honorary doctorate degrees were conferred on several renowned figures in the society and the academia, including Ja-kyung Kim (28.5.94), Gyeong-ri Park (27.8.94), Won-yong Kang (26.8.95), Sun-ae Kim (31.5.96), Il-whan Kim (31.5.96) and Rev. Heung-ho Kim (31.5.96).

To undertake memorial projects for former school presidents, President Yoon formed the Kim Okgill Memorial Project Committee (chairperson: Se-young Kim) on March 19, 1993, and named the lecture hall at Mokdong Hospital the Kim Okgill Memorial Hall. She also published a collection of Kim's sermons under the title *My Cup Overflows* and posthumous works under the title *The Open Gate and a Bowl of Cold Noodles*. Chairperson Chung Ii-sook meanwhile established the annual "Kim Okgill Memorial Lecture" with 1 billion won contributed by the school foundation.

February 27, 1999, marked the 100th anniversary of the birth of Dr. Helen Kim. Yoon had early announced on plans for a memorial project (10.2.95) and began preparations. Commemorating Helen Kim's birthday on February 27, 1996, an exhibition of Kim's works and personal articles was held, and a memorial anthology titled *A life Victorious : Can You Hear the Voices?* was published. Yoon passed the baton for future memorial projects to the next school president who served as chairperson of the committee.

Many efforts were made during this time to strengthen the University's relationship and collaborative ties with the alumnae. Ewha graduates were frequently invited to participate in a variety of school functions and events, and in cooperation with the office of the University chaplain, alumnae Gospel meetings started to be held in April 1994. The school and alumnae now hold a joint Christmas service at the Welch-Ryang Auditorium every year. In addition, Ewha alumnae were encouraged to organize meetings by different areas of profession to promote friendship and exchange, and the alumnae association held a celebration to recognize significant achievements of Ewha graduates.

Various measures were introduced to improve the personnel management system, work performance system and employee welfare for the school's administrative staff. These measures included: improving the rank promotion system, pay scale and holiday leaves (1991, 1992) ; holding regular meetings between managers and the section heads of office staff (March 92) ; introducing monthly leaves, annual leaves and paid holidays (September 93) ; hiring by open recruitments (February 94) ; instituting a functional job classification system, a reward and recognition system, job performance evaluation system, a grievance procedure, and internal and external training programs (April 94); introducing merit rating system (March 95) and introducing the job rotation system (September 95).

In 1995, Ewha and 22 other prestigious private universities in the country were evaluated by the Korean Council for University Education. Since the Council was formed in 1982, its proprietary functions has been the evaluation of universities. This comprehensive evaluation and accreditation process is aimed at promoting the quality and development of Korean universities. The first round of evaluations took place in the period between 1994 to 2000 during which schools were evaluated on 100 items in six areas — education, research, social contribution, faculty, facilities and equipment, and finance and administration.

Ewha was evaluated from the 23rd to 25th of October, 1995, during which an eight-member evaluation committee spent three days on campus. When the results of the evaluations were announced, Ewha was ranked first among all of the universities in the country, a result that even Ewha did not expect. It was an official recognition that firmly placed Ewha's leading position and a reaffirmation that Ewha's dedication and hard work over the past 110 years had not been in vain.

Upon completion of their assessment of the University, the evaluation committee made a deep impression with the following remarks : 1) "Ewha is a truly outstanding school," 2) "Ewha's educational quality proved itself to be extraordinarily high" 3) "Ewha is a school of great integrity and honesty", and 4) "Ewha is a school that deserves prestige and recognition."

Afterwards, President Yoon started a fund-raising campaign and successfully raised 73 billion won in two years. These funds were used to construct new buildings and upgrade existing facilities, which enabled Ewha to accelerate its development. Such achievements were founded on the insight and vision of the Ewha's leaders.

The Grand Vision of Ewhaians : Helping Women to Shape the Future

In 1996, Ewha celebrated its 110th anniversary. Throughout its history Ewha has always stood at the forefront of a new age, blending traditional

7. Ewha - On the Road to Becoming a World-Renowned University in the 21st Century (1990-1996)

values with the new.

In her congratulatory address, President Yoon proclaimed that, in order to succeed this grand tradition, all efforts would be made to earn Ewha an undisputed position as a world-renowned university. She emphasized that Ewha must play a leading role in linking education to culture, to science and technology, and to economics and politics and in restoring the nation's homogeneity; it must become a leading force in Korea for the sake of peace in northeast Asia; it must become a leading force in forming a community of peace for the sake of all humankind; and it must become a standard bearer in breaking down distinctions in the roles between men and women. She also reiterated that Ewha's eternal mission and role is to be a source of life, light and salvation.

A large concert was held in the athletic field to celebrate the school's 110th anniversary on May 30. Tens of thousands of members of the Ewha family including students, graduates and their young children, and even some alumnae who had graduated 60 years ago, gathered together in one place to watch the performances of Ewha alumnae who are now prominent figures on the international stage, the best vocalists in the country and the University choir. It was a great celebration in honor of what Ewha's achieved over the past 110 years, and it was a great occasion when all of Ewha came together as one.

In the 1996 student admission process, 12,949 students applied for 3,994 places. More outstanding female high school graduates than in any other year applied to study at Ewha. Of all successful applicants, 46.82% were in the 1st and 2nd level in terms of school records, and 35% ranked within the top 5% percent of college entrance exam scores. Such exceptional students joined the Ewha family. That year, Hyo-jeong Koo, who placed first in Scholastic Assessment Test of all female students across the country, expressed her feelings on entering Ewha as the head of the class in the

College of Business Administration : "I am happy to be able to study on a campus with no sexual discrimination, receiving the full support of the school. I want to study so I can work for social equity and help those who are in need and those who are living in the margins of our society."

In August 1996, President Yoon, who had taken the lead in the reform of Ewha, stepped down upon expiration of her six-year term, expressing her gratitude to God who gave permission to dedicate herself for Korean women and Ewha. She also thanked the faculty, who had devoted themselves to Ewha during her tenure.

She had established a vision for the 21st century, which is to turn Ewha from a leading Korean university to a world-renowned university, and laid the ideological and physical foundation for Ewha's advance in its second century. She was a leader who created the framework that enable Ewha to join the ranks of the world's most prestigious universities. President Yoon has left a clear mark in the history of Ewha and women's educations as a visionary leader and great teacher.

To pay tribute to Yoon's prominent leadership, her achievements and her devoted service to the school, the professors requested that Yoon be named an Honorary President. The motion was passed through the foundation which agreed unanimously to the idea and at Yoon's retirement ceremony foundation Chairperson Chung Ii-sook gave Yoon a letter of appointment as Honorary President.

Index

A

Academic Research Institute for Ewha College and Ewha Kindergarten Training School   69, 70

Academic Research Institute for Law and Economics   70

accomplished scholarship system   128

Ada Prayer Room   68

Ahn, Gi-young   61, 64

Ahn, Chung-song → Lee, Salom

Ah-ryoung Dang (Home Management House)   116

Allen, Horace N.   23

Alumnae Building   116

Alumnae Queen   97

Appenzeller, Alice   46

Appenzeller Hall (Science Hall)   86, 139

Appenzeller, Henry G.   23, 46

Appenzeller sundial   139

April Uprising (April 19 Movement)   95

Armistice negotiation   86

Asan Hall (the Engineering Building)   125, 138

the Asian Center for Women's Studies   135

Australian Presbyterian Church   60

B

bachelor's degree holders as transfer students   132

Baejae Boys' school   46

Baker, Catherine   63, 64
Baldwin, L. B.   21
Baltimore Women's Medical College   26
Beijing University   125, 133
Benton   23
Billingsley Hall   87
Billings, Peggy   97, 98
Board of Trustees of Ewha Haktang   57, 74, 75
Bogu Yeogwan (The hospital only for women)   17, 26, 27
Boston University   40, 44, 47
branch associations   97
Bumindong   86
Bureau of School Affairs   84
Busan   81, 86, 87
Business Administration Building   116
Byeol-dan   25

C

campus-wide computer network   137
Canadian Presbyterian Church   60
Case hall of Music   68
Centennial ceremony   118
center of learning and research-focused university   112, 114, 132
Ceramic Research Institute   116
Chae, Sun-yop   64, 73
chairperson of Ewha Haktang Board of Trustees   44
Cho, Hyun-kyong   72
Cho, Jung-hwan   64
Cho, Soon   128

Choi, Byeong-wook   129

Choi, Esther   29

Choi, Helen   20, 29, 39, 40, 43

Choi, Hyun-bae   63

Choi, I-kwon   72

Choi, Ii-soon   65, 73

Choi, Keum-bong → Choi, Me-jee

Choi, Me-jee (Choi, Keum-bong)   44

Choi, Shin-duk   72

Choi, Sun-hwa   72

Christian universities   48

Chu, Tae-kyoung   57, 75

Chung, Ae-shik → Kim, Ae-shik

Chung, Ii-sook   99, 105, 109, 110, 112, 113, 118, 120, 127, 139, 140, 144

Chung, In-bo   61, 63

Chung, In-sup   84

Chung, Geun-mo   130

Chung, Hoon-mo   64

Chung, Hwa-young   64

Chung, Kyung-wha   140

Chung, Myung-wha   140

Chung, Myung-whun   140

Chungjeong Building   138

Church, Marie E.   42

Classical Chinese   28, 39, 40, 69, 74

Clara Hall   68

The Collection of Essays in Celebration of the 80th Anniversary   97

the College at Ewha Haktang   34, 36, 38, 46, 51

the College of Academics   85

the College of Art 85
the College of Business Administration 144
the College of Education 116, 140
the College of Engineering 125, 129, 130, 133
the College of Home Economics 102
the College of Law 87, 134
the College of Liberal Arts 134
the College of Medicine 85, 136, 137, 138
the College of Medicine's Sudong-myeon Community Health Center 138
the College of Natural Science 116
the Colleges of Pharmacy 132
the College of Social Science 132, 134
Columbia University 44, 47, 79
Committee for Faculty promotion 87
Committee to work out centennial projects 117
community service 108, 132, 136
Computer Research Center 113, 114
Conrow, Marion 63
Corea, the Hermit Nation 22
Course evaluation system 134
Czoj, Halina Ogarek 128

D

Dallet, Charles 22
Demeron, Josephine 64
Department of Architecture 133
Department of Early Childhood Education 85
Department of Computer Science 135
Department of English Language and Literature 56, 109

Index

Department of Environmental Science   133
Department of Fine Arts   85
Department of General Education   58, 87
Department of Home Economics   59, 62, 64, 65, 73, 85
Department of Information Electronics Engineering   133
Department of Korean Studies   113
Department of Law   101
Department of Leadership Training for Young Women   76
Department of Literature   56, 58. 63, 85
Department of Medicine   76, 85
Department of Music   34, 53, 58
Department of Pharmacy   85
Department of Physical Education   85
Department of Women Studie   113
Devotion League   42
Dongdaemun Hospital   138
Dongdaemoon Women's Hospital   76
Donghak   22
Dongnip Shinmun (The Independent)   24
dormitory   18, 19, 29, 41, 66, 115, 139
dual majors   132, 126

E

Edae Hakbo (the weekly Ewha)   88
Education Hall → Emma Hall   116
Educational Multimedia Center   134
Educational Research   86
The *80 Years History of Ewha*   97
The *80th Anniversary Commemorative Illustrated Book*   97

Emerson Chapel   68
Emerson, Fannie G.   67
Emma Hall (Education Hall)   116
Engineering Building → Asan Hall
English Practice House   63, 68
Eunji-ri   130
Evacuee Campus   81, 86, 87
Ewha (the literary journal)   66
Ewha Alumnae Association   43
Ewha Alumnae Writers' Association   72
Ewha Academy   130
Ewha Academy of Science   130
Ewha Bridge   87, 139
Ewha Broadcasting Academy   134
Ewha Campus Network   138
Ewha Centennial Library   107, 116, 118
Ewha Centennial Museum   116
Ewha College and Ewha Kindergarten Training School Catalogue   69
Ewha color broadcasting station   134
Ewha Color Design Institute   135
Ewha Development Master Plan   119
Ewha Development Task Force Committee   119
Ewha Faculty Reasearch Fund   112
Ewha High School → the high school
Ewha Institute for Professional Certification   134
Ewha Institute for Women's Theological Studies   135
Ewha Integrated Information System (E.T.I.S.)   138
Ewha intellect   110
Ewha Kindergarten   39, 71, 114, 116

Index

Ewha Kindergarten Training School   34, 39, 44, 55, 59, 61, 68, 69, 70, 71, 73, 74
Ewha Legal Science Institute   135
Ewha Medical Camp   137
Ewha-POSCO Building   115, 139
Ewha-Samsung Culture Center   138
Ewha school song   60, 61
Ewha-SK Telecom Center   138
Ewha Sosik (Ewha News)   136
Ewha Ten-year Development Plan   91, 97, 100
Ewha 21st Century Development Patrons Committee   130
Ewha 21st Century Development Plan   120, 130
Ewha 21st Century Development Planning Committee   130
Ewha Weekly News Sheet   60
Ewha Womans University Archives   108, 114, 115
Ewha Womans University Cooperating Board in North America   98
Ewha Y.W.C.A. (Young Women's Christian Association)   43, 65, 66
Ewha's seven-member evangelical mission   37, 42
Ewha's vision for the 21st century   131, 144
Ewha Voice   88
Experimental University   98, 99, 100

F

faculty exchange programs   102
Faculty Meetings of the Ewha College and Ewha Kindergarten Training School   61
father of the Haktang   27
Federation of Missionary Organization   48
Fine Arts Building   139
Finger, Mamie Lee   98

151

Frey Hall   36, 41, 46, 47, 66, 68
Frey, Lulu E.   33, 40, 45, 46, 72
friends of Ewha   87, 116
fund-raising campaign   67, 97, 130, 142

G

Gae, Joon-tae   72
Gae, Jung-sik   64
Gaewha sasang (Enlightenment thoughts)   22
Gapsin Jeongbyeon : The Coup d'Etat of 1884   23
Gatsui women's school   40
general meeting of Christian women's universities of Asia   99
globalization   128, 129, 130, 131, 132
graduate quota system   106, 111, 115
Graduate School of Clinical Health Sciences   136
Graduate School Credit Exchange Program   102
Graduate School of Industrial Design   113, 114
Graduate School of Information Science   136
Graduate school of International Studies   136
Graduate School of Law   136
Graduate School of Policy Sciences   136
Graduate School of Social Welfare   136, 137
Graduate School of Theology   136
Graduate School of Translation and Interpretation   136
Gray, Philip H.   47, 72
Griffith, William Elliot   22
Gützlaff, Karl   22
Gyeongseong Women's College   76
gym skirt (*Jokki-hurri*)   35, 41

H

Haansoft   138

Haenig, Hulda A.   40

Hah, Bok-soon   44

Hah, Ran-sa   29, 30, 39

Hakkwan (Korean-American Hall)   87, 139

Han, Chi-jin   64

Han, Suh-rin   45

Hanisol Building (Foundation Building)   138

Hanwoori Hall (new domitory)   139

Harmon, Grace   40

Helen Hall   87

Heungsun Daewongun   22

the high school (Ewha High School)   68, 71

History of Chosun (Joseon)   22

Home Management House   68, 116

Hong, Aesiduk   42

Hongpadong   63

honor professor   128

Honorary President   144

Howard, Meta   26

Hrubos, Ildiko   128

Hulbert, Jeanette   75

Human Ecology Environmental Institute   135

Humanities Hall (Faculty Building)   138

Hwang, Esther   44

Hwang, Eung-yeon   128, 129

Hwang, Jae-kyoung   64

Hwang, Me-re   30

Hwang, On-soon   45

I

Ilyeop (Kim, Won-ju)   44
Independence Movement   42, 43, 44
Induk College   43
information technology   129, 130, 132, 135
Institute for International Trade and Cooperation   135
Institute of Bioscience   113, 135
Institute of Language Education   114, 137
integrated woman   127
International Education Institute   114, 132
International Foundation For Ewha Womans University, INC   97, 98
International Hall   139
International Prayer Fellowship Conference   97
International Summer School   102
Introduction to the History of Korean Church   22

J

Jemulpo   23
Jeon, Doo-hwan   111
Jeon, Sin-ae   140
Jeon, Sook-hee   72
Jeongdong   23, 25, 46, 54, 55, 68, 69, 75
Jeongdong Methodist Church   25, 46
Jinsunmi Hall   68, 139
Joseon   22, 23, 24, 26, 48, 116
Joseon Education Decree   48
Jung, Choong-ryang   72

K

Kang, Kyung-shik   129

Kang, Sung-hee   72

Kang, Won-yong   140

Kansas at Ewha Program   102

Kansas University   102

Katmandu   137

Kim, Ae-eun   42

Kim, Ae-shik (Ae-shik Chung, Alice Kim)   34, 39, 43

Kim, Alice → Kim, Ae-shik

Kim, Bae-young   44

Kim, Bok-hee   45

Kim, Emma   45, 84, 140

Kim, Hap-na   42, 65

Kim, Helen   42, 44, 47, 57, 64, 67, 74, 75, 79, 84, 88, 95, 96, 97, 98, 118, 129, 140

Kim, Heung-ho   140

Kim, Il-soon   72

Kim, Il-whan   140

Kim, Im-sun   140

Kim, In-young   64

Kim, Ja-kyung   140

Kim, Jeom-dong → Park, Esther

Kim, Jessie   29

Kim, Jin-hae   72

Kim, Joon-sup   84

Kim, Jung-ok   72

Kim, Kap-soon   72

Kim, Me-re   43

Kim, Mary   64, 72
Kim, Okgill   84, 91, 96, 97, 100, 101, 109, 140
Kim Okgill Memorial Hall   140
Kim Okgill Memorial Lecture   140
Kim Okgill Memorial Project Committee   140
Kim, Pauline   42
Kim, Seok-jun   130
Kim, Se-young   140
Kim, Shin-do   42
Kim, Shin-shil   62
Kim, Soon-ae   73
Kim, Won-bok   64
Kim, Won-ju → Ilyeop
Kim, Young-Ii   64, 84
King, Gojong   17, 25
The King's Daughters   42
Kkon-nim   24, 25
Koo, Hyo-jeong   143
Korea Institute of Science and Technology (K.I.S.T.)   133
Korea-U.S. Treaty of Amity and Commerce   23, 25
Korean-American Cooperative Board of Trustees   74
Korean-American Hall → Hakkwan
Korean Council for University Education (the former University Education Council of Korea)   141
Korean Cultural Research Institute   88, 113
Korean Patriotic Women's Society   44
Korean Research Institute for Better Living   113
Koreans to worship the Shinto Shrine   75
Korean War   81, 82, 86, 140

Korean Women's Institute   100, 101, 113, 135

Kosa-ri Retreat Center   116, 117

Kwak, Sung-sil   45

Kwon, Kyoung-joo   129, 139

L

Lamb, Susan Rubby   98

Law and Political Science Building   116

Lee, Charlotte Georgia Brown   40

Lee, Dorothy   34, 39, 43

Lee, Eun-ra   39, 64

Lee, Eun-sang   63

Lee, Hee-seung   63

Lee, Hyo-jae   140

Lee, In-ho   128

Lee, Jong-tae   64

Lee, Jung-ae   84

Lee, Jung-koo   84

Lee, Jung-sook   72

Lee, Kyong-sook   27

Lee, Ou-ryung   129

Lee, Pong-soon   72

Lee, Salom (Ahn, Chung-song)   44

Lee, Soo-jung   21

Lee, So-ran   72

Lee, Sung-hee   63

Lee, Tae-joon   63

Lee, Tae-young   73

Lee, Won-sook   140

Lessons on the Human Body   18, 28
the Liberal Arts Education Committee   100
A life Victorious: Can You Hear the Voices?   141
Lim, Bessie   44
Lim, Gil-jae   140
Lim, Sang-hee   64
Literary Society   43, 56

M

Maengsan   96
Main Hall   29, 37
March 1st Movement of 1919   66
May Queen   20, 54, 62, 88, 97, 102
Maynor, Velma H.   63
Mazur, U. N.   128
McLaren, C. I.   68
Medical Research Center   135
Medical Research Institute   138
Memorial Lecture for Helen Kim   129
merit-rating system   114
Microsoft   138
the middle school   27, 28, 29, 30, 44, 84
military coup d'etat of May 16, 1961   95
military sexual slavery   140
Ministry of Education   80, 85, 86, 100, 133, 136
Missionary Society   15, 21, 23, 42, 47, 57, 74, 98
Mitchell, Betty   98
Mo, Yun-suk   72
Mokdong Hospital   124, 136, 138, 140

Index

Moon, Grace   29
Morris, Harriett P.   65
Museum   18, 47, 70, 87, 108, 116, 118, 137, 138
Museum of Natural History   138
Music Building   139
Music Institute of Ewha Womans University   135
My Cup Overflows   140

N

nationwide test qualifying bachelor's degree holders   95
Natural History Museum   137
Nepal   137
Network Development Committee   138
new Pharmaceutical Science Building   138
The New York Times   98
Noh, Chun-myung   72
Northwestern University   26, 40, 109, 127

O

Office of Academic Administration   100
Office of Admissions   137
Office of Planning and Coordination   136
Office of the University chaplain   141
Office of University Relations and Development   137
Ohio Wesleyan University   29, 39
100 challenges   127, 130, 131
The 100 Years History of Ewha   131, 132
The 100 Years of Ewha Historical Documents and Artifacts   131
the 100th anniversary commemoration song   119

159

The Open gate and a Bowl of cold Noodles　140
open recruitment system　134

P

Pageant of the May Queen　88, 102
Paik, Nak-joon　64
Paine, Josephine O.　27
Park, Chung-hee　110
Park, Esther (Kim, Jeom-dong)　25, 26, 27
Park, Eun-hae　72
Park, Gyeong-ri　140
Park, In-duk　42, 43
Park, Jong-hong　64
Park, Kyung-ho　64
Park, Maria　72
Pang, Shin-young　65
Park, Woo-dong　129
patriotic movement　66
pear blossom　25, 116
Pfeiffer Hall　68
Pfeiffer, Henry G.　67
plans for a Christian women's university　47, 48
Pohang University of Science and Technology　133
Posture Queen　54, 62
the preparatory college　40
the primary school　29
principal　15, 26, 27, 33, 36, 39, 40, 46, 47, 57
Proud Ewha Alumna Award　139, 140
Public Relations Office　136

Purity League   42
Pye, Olive F.   40
Pyun, Young-ro   63

R

The Regulations of Ewha College   69
Regulations of Ewha Haktang as a Private School   39
The Regulations of Ewha Kindergarten Training School   69
Reorganization Preparatory Committee   129
Research Club for Philosophy   64
Research Institute of Basic Science   113, 135
Research Institute of Natural History   135
retreat of January   86
revival meeting   88, 97
Rhee Syng-man   95
The River (a play about the history of Ewha)   71
Ross, John   22
Rothweiler, Louisa Christina   26
Rules on Private Schools (1911)   38
Rural Education for the Regeneration of Korea   44
Ryoo, Kwan-yol   84

S

sabbatical system   128
Scholastic Assessment Test   143
School of Continuing Education   114, 137
school emblem   60
school motto of "Truth, Goodness and Beauty"   60
science   128, 129, 130, 132, 133

Science Building   116, 138

Science Hall → Appenzeller Hall

Scranton, Mary Fletcher   15, 23

Scranton, William B.   23

Scranton, William T.   23

Sears, Kathryne   98

seminars of the Literature Department   70

a series of books on Korean culture   118

Sherwood, Rosetta   26

Shin, Ei-kyung   72

Shin, Joon-ryeo   43

Shin, Marcella   34, 39, 43

The sister university program   132

Sohn, Myung-soon   139

Sohn, Chang-sik   75

Sohn, In-shil   72

Songjuk League   44

Sontag Hotel   36, 39

South Methodist Episcopal Church   60

South Pyongan province   96

specialized departments   84

Speech and Hearing Center   114

Stevens, Susanne L.   98

Stover, Myrta   62

Student Union Building   138

students' organization   43, 60

Sudong-myeon Community Health Center   138

Sung, Rak-su   64

super-woman syndrome   101

Supporters' Association for Ewha College   74, 75
the system of research students   69
the system of choosing one's major in the second year   114
the system of selective course registrant   70
the system of transferred students.   69

T

Taylor, Mark Klino   128
Teaching Assistants   113
Temple University   96
Ten-year Development Supporters' Association   97
The Ten-year Development Plan Supporters' Association   97
Thomas Gymnasium   68
training center for nurses   26, 27
Treaty of Annexation in 1910   38
Troxel, Moneta J.   64
trusteeship   84

U

Underwood, Horace G.   23
University Church   139
University Development Committee   129
University Development Planning Committee   128, 129
University Restructuring Law   95

V

Van Fleet, Edna M.   64, 67
volunteer work for Academic Credits   137

W

Walter, A. Jeannette   40, 47, 87
Warsaw University   128, 133
wartime union of college   86
Welch-Ryang Auditorium   83, 87, 88, 101, 139, 141
welfare   129, 130
Wellesley College   46
Wesleyan University   29, 39, 96
Wijeong cheoksa   22
Wilke, Julia   98
Women's Foreign Missionary Society (WFMS)   15, 21, 23, 47, 57, 59, 67
Women's Supreme Leadership Course   136
women's studies   45, 93, 100, 109, 113, 127, 130, 135
Won, Hee-deuk   84
Wood, Grace   75
Woowol Anthology   118
a world-renowned university   123, 127, 129, 131, 133, 143, 144

Y

Yang, Han-na   45
Yoon, Hoo Jung   101, 127, 139
Yoon, Il-sun   84
Yoon, Sung-duk   42
Young Hwa Primary School in Incheon   44
Young, Mary   61, 64